How To Use Periscope For Small Business

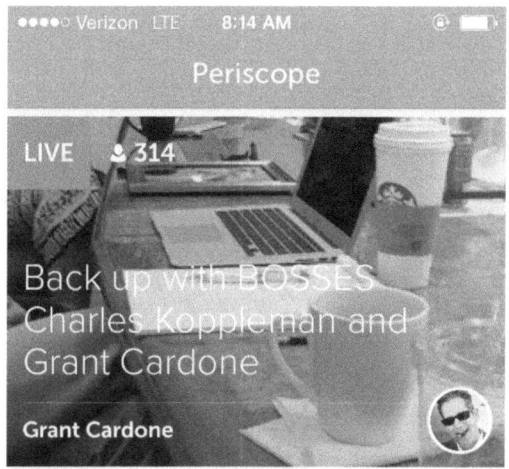

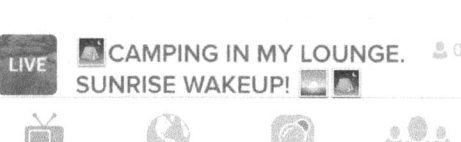

Volume 2

By Darrell White

@carteblancheme (Professional)

@motivating_mins (personal)

@darrellrwhite_

Want to join a community of people learning how to navigate Periscope? Join the Facebook group:

https://www.facebook.com/groups/Periscopetipsntricks

Special Thanks to Ruthy Otero for gracing the cover.

 @RuthyOtero

Section 1:
Periscope Basics

In this section we'll go over the basics of how to use Periscope both as an observer and content creator. The introduction includes basic information on how Periscope came about and the author's own Journey with Periscope.

By "basics" we mean how to navigate through the app both as an audience member and as a content creator.

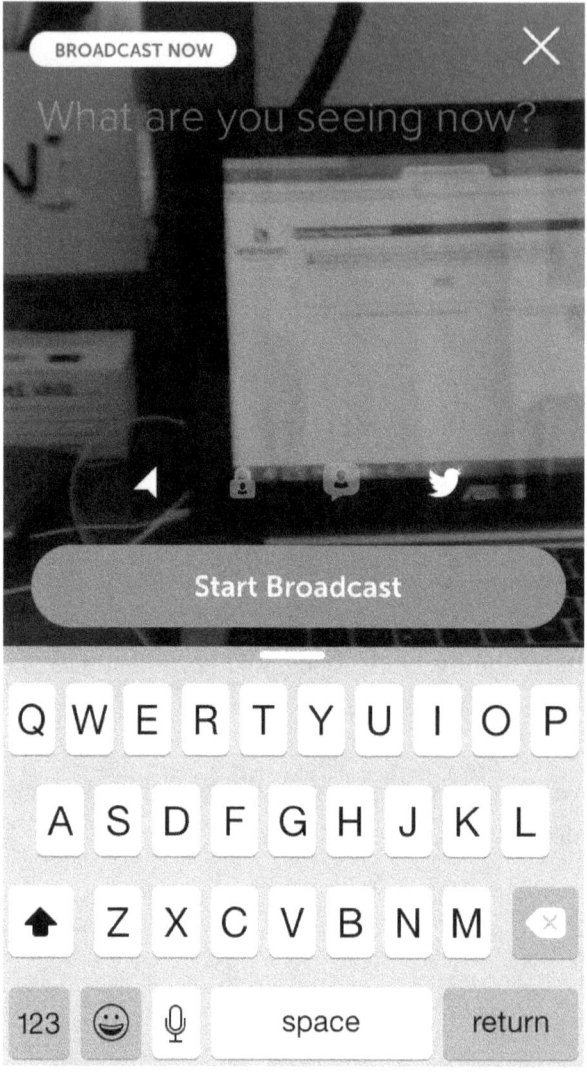

At the end of this section you should be able to do all of the following:

A. Navigate through the periscope app as a viewer

B. Curate – or identify Broadcasters that you like – on Periscope

C. Broadcast – learn how to broadcast you and/or your business

Introduction: What is Periscope? + My Periscope Journey

Q: **So What is Periscope?**
A: Periscope is one of two live-streaming apps (the other named Meerkat) that debuted at the SouthbySouthwest Conference in Austin, TX in March of 2015.

Q: How many people are on Periscope?
A: The exact figures change daily but as of this writing there are approximately 3.7 4.3 5.9 million Periscope followers of the Periscope app (@periscopeco) itself – this is the first profile automatically followed by every periscope user. In August 2015 AdWeek reported that Periscope had 10 million users.

Q: How did you get on Periscope?
A: I got on Periscope like a lot of things in life by way of painful humiliation followed by a great discovery. I was attending the New Media Expo #NMX– an internet marketing conference (formerly named Blogworld) that is focused on Content Creation.

Unfortunately, the Friday before the conference I lost my Android smartphone and not wanting to pay additional expenses at the conference I opted to reactivate my old slider phone with hopes that a simple laptop would work for keeping connected at the conference.

As anyone who attends an internet marketing conference should know, this was a mistake on my part.

At an evening event I asked one of my conversation partners for their card. Fresh out, they advised I simply save their information onto my phone. Not thinking, I pulled out said slider phone and…. laughter ensued…all around.

Needless to say, the next day my first task was to buy a phone created within the last year. The only store open early enough for me to get a phone and attend a key seminar at the conference was the Apple store. So, I purchased a brand new IPhone. Later that day much of the talk in between events focused on this "new" Periscope App that had just launched at the "Southby" conference. Luck would have it – the app was only available for the IPhone at the time and a new passion was born.

Since that date, I have

- Broadcast over ~~250~~ ~~270~~ 600 times
- Accumulated over ~~11,000~~ ~~15,000~~ 91,000 hearts
- Accumulated over ~~150~~ ~~260~~ 600 followers on the app
- Increased my Twitter following from approximately 260 followers to over ~~800~~ 1400
- Spoke on Periscope to a live audience and currently scheduled to speak at 3 local venues
- Watched sunsets and sunrises from every coast imaginable
- Taught (several) dozens of people unfamiliar with the app what it does and how to use it
- Made several virtual friends amongst the #perifamily – some local – some across the globe.

Chapter 1 - Watching others

one of Joe Polish's (@joepolish) early Periscopes

Watching others on Periscope is likely the first place you want to start when using the app. Unless you are an experienced YouTube, Vimeo or Vine personality - it makes the most sense to observe a number of broadcasts before you begin to broadcast yourself.

To be honest, even if you are an experienced YouTuber or other video platform star, there is definitely a different way people interact when livestreaming then they do on video that is edited and then uploaded.

You will likely pick up on a number of things that work for broadcasters and things that don't work as well for less experienced broadcasters.

When you first log in to the app you will see a screen similar to the following (if you have an IPhone) Android screens look much different:

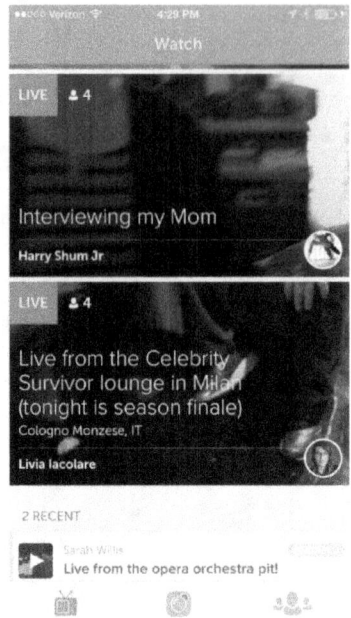

One key difference you'll find is that currently the bottom navigation has 4 icons instead of the 3 shown above. We'll share examples of both the "4 icon" screen and an Android screen shortly within this book.

For the purposes of instruction please review the image above again. You'll notice that there are 3 selections you are forced to make for your initial settings.

We would suggest that you choose to definitely

- Enable the camera function
- Enable the microphone function

We would caution you on activating the 3rd choice "Location" unless you are in a very public location as the location function is extremely accurate. We'll discuss that a little more in a later chapter.

As mentioned here is what the different screens typically look like once you have selected your initial default settings for the camera,

microphone and location.

Let's take a look at the navigation icons briefly before going into each one more individually. We'll start from the right and move left.

Leaderboard aka "Three Amigos"

This screen allows you to do a number of things that will impact your periscope experience. The first of which is to make changes to your own personal Periscope Profile.

For IPhone users: You can change your bio/description. Unfortunately, you cannot yet change your name (if you signed up using your Twitter account). If you sign up using Twitter your photo will be the same as what is on your Twitter account.

For Android users: You can change both your description and also apparently your photo and name on Periscope – assuming you signed up using a Twitter account.

●●●○○ Verizon 📶 12:03 AM ⚫ ▭▭+

D@Motivatingminutes
♥ 6,635

Prior: #yelper #nationwider
#cubicledwlr Now: #blogger
#socialmedia #entrepreneur

Following   620 >

Followers   160 >

Blocked   0 >

Broadcasts   180 >

As you can see above, the leaderboard icon will also allow you to see

- How many followers you have
- How many people you are following
- How many people you've blocked
- How many Broadcasts that you've done

Profile

To get to your own profile from the leaderboard simply tap on the profile head in the top right hand corner of your screen.

Search

When you are on the Leaderboard/"Three Amigos" section you will notice in the upper left hand section there is a magnifying glass icon. This icon is the search function of Periscope.

You can use this primarily to search for things like:

- People or Profiles you are not currently following on Twitter but may be on a list
- Interests that are relevant to you based on Hashtags
- People or profiles in similar industries to you
- People in the same or nearby geographic locations to you, Etc.

Following on Twitter

This will be the first screen you see when you highlight the "Leaderboard/Three Amigos" section of the account.

As the title suggests – these are people who you follow on Twitter who are now on Periscope as well. A good practice is to check this list weekly or daily depending on how many people you follow as new names arrive daily.

Leaderboard/Three Amigos

So underneath the "FOLLOWING ON TWITTER" section you will find the Heart Leaderboard or "MOST LOVED" section.

As the title suggests these are the "heart" leaders or the people that have been liked the most on Periscope.

A QUICK NOTE ON HEARTS

Hearts are the equivalent to "likes" on Facebook. You can create a heart by simply tapping on a screen as our viewing a broadcast. One key difference to hearts on Periscope and "likes" on other platforms is that you can give a broadcaster up to 500 "hearts" in one viewing. You can also "X" out or logout of broadcast and come back and deliver more hearts to a broadcaster as well.

HEARTFRAUD CAUTION: One thing I and other broadcasters have experienced – especially when their profile is relatively new – is a possible conflict with what is likely an algorithm that deletes new, unexpected hearts from the record.

For example: I once broadcasted on my newer periscope profile @carteblancheme – had one of my followers from my other profile @Motivating_mins join my broadcast and she immediately began tapping her screen to show appreciation for the scope. By the end of the scope I counted at least 800 hearts given by my fellow broadcaster. However, the next day when I checked – only 6 hearts registered. I reached out to Twitter and Periscope about the removal and within the day the 6 hearts were replaced with about 100 hearts.

A friend had a similar experience and tells me that he accumulated 10,000 hearts in the course of about a half hour broadcast but the next day he only had a handful (less than 100) hearts to show for the hearts accumulated. All this leads me to believe that Twitter and/or the Periscope team has an algorithm in place to prevent people from doing things like buying 3 phones, broadcasting from 1 and simply tapping or having a friend tap indiscriminately on their phones using the other 2 phones.

Thus, Gaming the system in this way has already been thought through it seems and the powers that be can and will block what they see as irregularities as a result.

Chapter 2 –
Curating Scopes you would like to watch

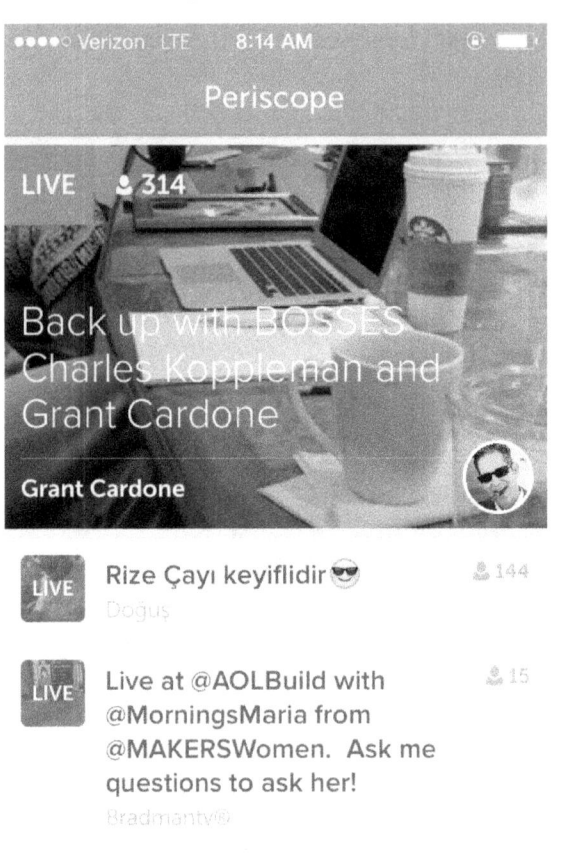

The above screenshot has the TV or subscription section highlighted.

The TV icon on the far left of your navigation is for viewing broadcasts from profiles that you subscribe to. Occasionally, especially if you follow few profiles, there will appear broadcasts that you might find interesting.

Globe

The Globe Icon is the best way to find new Periscope channels is to follow and also utilize the MAP function to see who is broadcasting near you. The List function is available on both the Apple and Android platforms.

Map View (only available on Apple IOS -as of this writing)

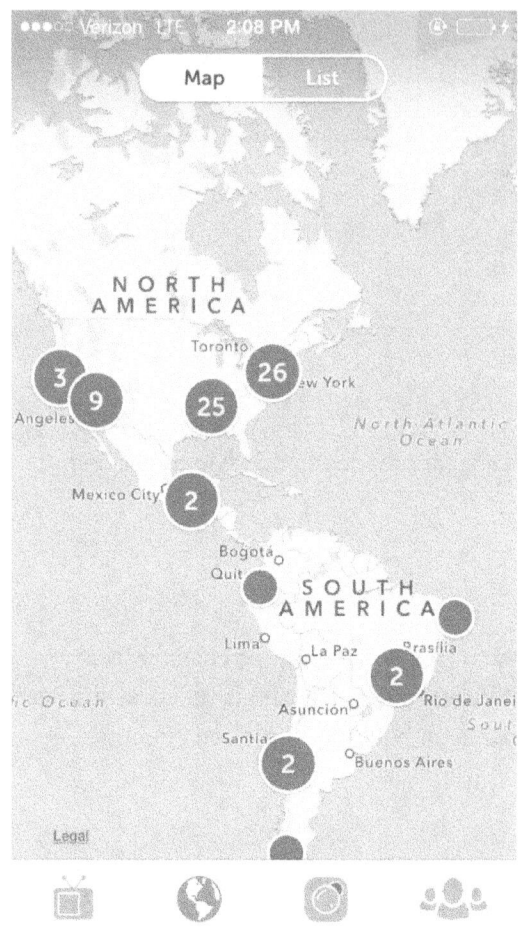

The Map View was just released for the IPhone version as of June 2015. This view is very powerful as it can zoom in from a country view, down to a state view and in some cases get as close as the nearest street corner someone is broadcasting from.

This is the exact reason I would be wary turning on this function when you decide to broadcast – especially if you are doing so from home.

List View

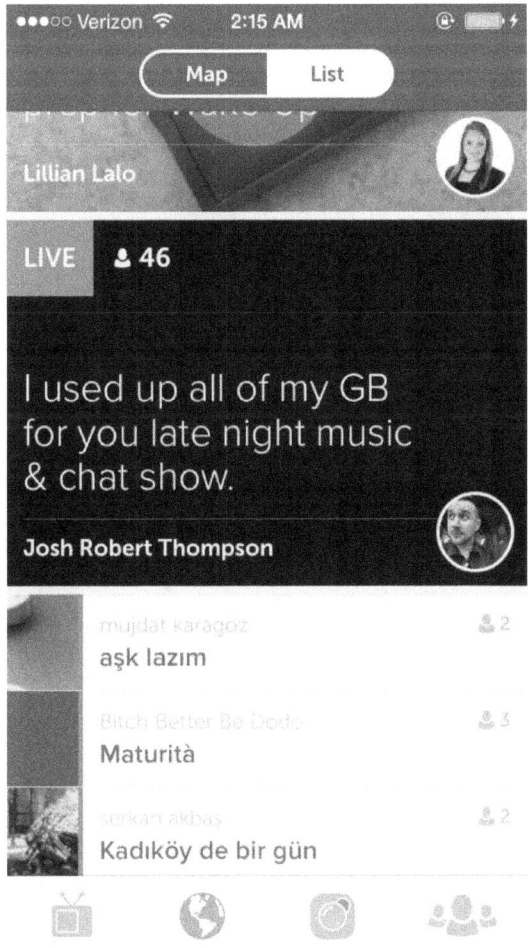

The above is what the list view looks like

The list view is a great way to search for people by title and their thumbnail alone. The thumbnail is short hand for the picture that shows to represent the broadcast.

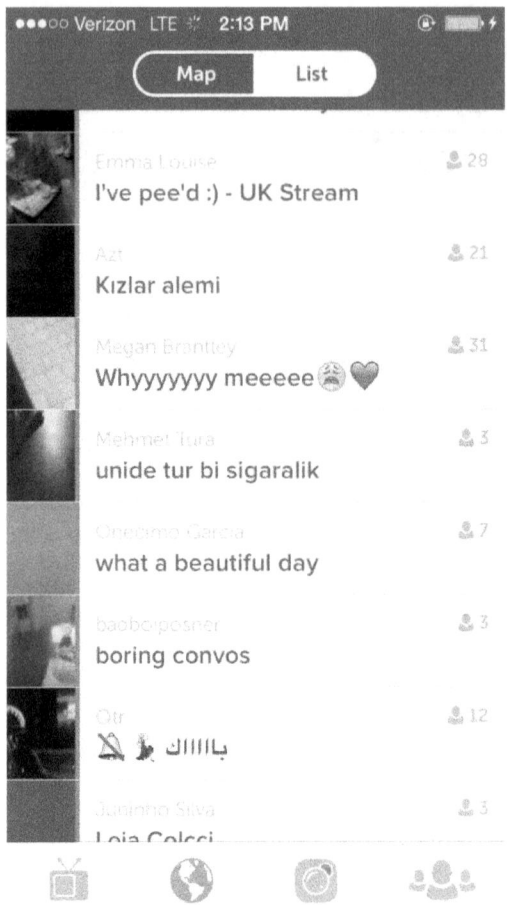

This is what the LIST version looks like currently.

Once you have watched a few broadcasts (or "scopes" as they're described within the community) you can begin to determine what type of broadcasters talk to what you like to view and what is interesting to you.

This is also when you will begin to curate and start to follow certain broadcasters and avoid others. This leads to the curation piece of Periscope.

Curate

You can find out more information about different broadcasters by simply tapping on the number of viewers icon as you watch a broadcast.

Additionally, you can swipe right on Apple IOS or Swipe up on Android phones to find additional information. You can check the top right hand corner of this brief description to follow the individual.

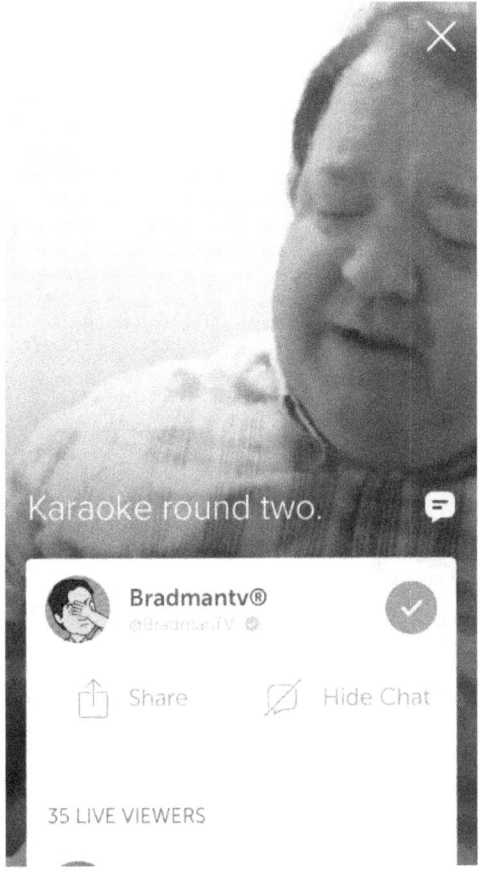

If you double tap on the broadcasters profile from this screen an even more detailed display of the broadcaster will appear.

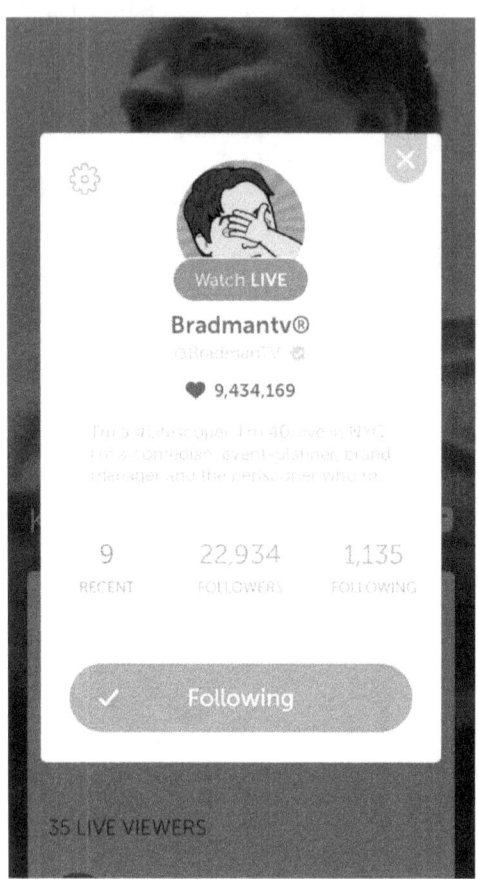

As you can see above this enhanced screen will allow you to read a full description of the broadcaster. It will allow you to see how many recent broadcasts they've done. How many followers the broadcaster has. Finally it will allow you to see how many people are currently following them.

Chapter 3 - Broadcasting Yourself

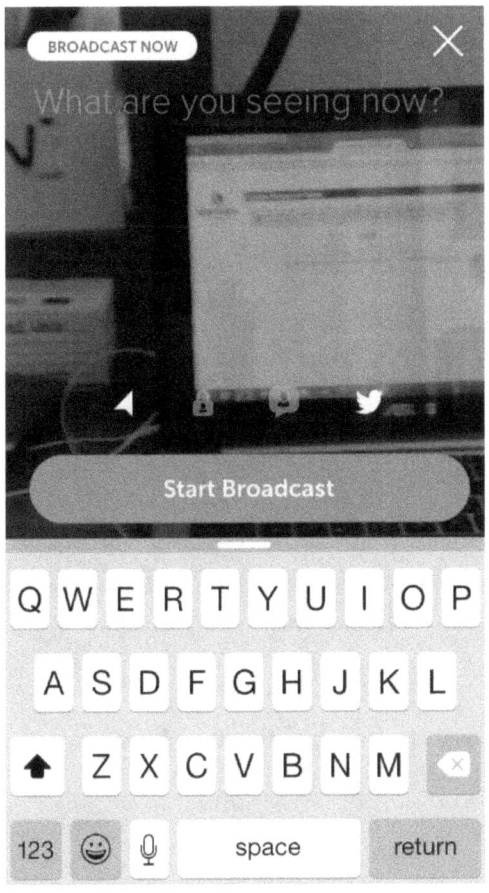

Eventually if you want to actively promote your business or yourself as a brand – you will have to start broadcasting. The Broadcasting option is located under the Lens or "monocle" navigation on the bottom middle right hand side of the navigation. The moment you press this navigation button the above screen will appear. Be aware – the moment you press the red "BROADCAST NOW" you will start sharing your world with THE world.

Broadcast Icons

So let's take a moment to discuss the different greyed out (or highlighted) icons you'll see immediately before you do your first broadcast.

Title

This is most likely the most important portion of your broadcast prep. It is unwise to simply hit "BROADCAST NOW" without setting a title. We'll discuss this a little more in further chapters. The lone exception to this is if you are celebrity of some sort and already have an active and engaged Twitter following.

Location

The arrowhead icon turns on or turns off the location function of your scope. If you are in a private location please be aware that the location function allows users to zoom in down to the street corner in some instances.

If you are in a public place or massive office building then by all means use this function.

LOCK

The LOCK icon limits your broadcasts to only either:

a) All of those currently following you

Or

B) A single or multiple specific people that are currently following you

COMMENTS

The Speaking bubble icon – with a profile within it - allows you to limit your comments to only those who currently follow you.

TWITTER

As you might've guessed, the Twitter bird outline simply allows you to share your broadcast on Twitter. Deactivating it makes sure that it is not shared on Twitter but it will still be live on Periscope for 24 hours. That being said, for a business owner I would not suggest deactivating the Twitter bird icon unless you are doing a broadcast that is NSFW – which you shouldn't be doing on your business periscope in the first place.

FRONT CAMERA/BACK CAMERA

You can toggle between the back camera – facing away from you. and the front camera – facing towards you – by simply tapping on your screen twice.

Section 2:
Mistakes to Avoid

In this section, I'll go over what I've found to be the top 5 major mistakes people have made when doing periscope broadcasts. You should avoid making these mistakes at all costs.

Chapter 4 – Mistake #1:

No title

Unless you're a celebrity – broadcasting without a title is possibly the biggest mistake you can make.

Here's why, when people are looking for 'scopes to tune into the thumbnail image may be very hard to see or determine. Your profile picture may be interesting enough to draw people in or it may not.

However, your title, whether in the viewers native language or not, will be massively important in whether you draw people in and allow them to learn more about you, your world and your product or service.

Without a title it is also unlikely that you will show up high or at all on the list function of the globe section of those currently broadcasting. Keep this in mind.

Chapter 5 – Mistake #2:

Waiting for the delay

One thing that you'll notice after you've done a few of your own broadcasts is that there is a 5 – 10 second delay between when you hit "Start broadcast" and when your first few followers begin to trickle into your broadcast. As of this writing the delay on Periscope's key competitor Meerkat stands at about 30-45 seconds.

Despite the fact that no one may be watching the moment you begin to broadcast, it is important to start talking to your audience right away. To say nothing until someone arrives on your broadcast is the equivalent of "dead air" in radio and TV terminology.

The key reason this is a mistake is that as long as you don't delete the broadcast once you've concluded – which you do have the ability to do – there will be the possibility that viewers can view you in the replay and see the "dead air" portion of your broadcast.

If they see this uneventful portion of your initial broadcast, there is little likelihood that they will stay around till the end of it.

Not greeting viewers (mistake 2.5*)

A related mistake to not waiting for the delay is not greeting the viewers as they begin to enter your broadcasting "room".

In my early days of broadcasting a fellow broadcaster who was viewing at the time related a story of exactly not what to do if you are a broadcaster. To protect the innocent I'll describe the two characters from the frame of "**New periscope broadcaster**" and " **New Periscope Viewer**":

New 'scope broadcaster "Hey guys I have something important to tell you – tell all of your followers to join"

New 'scope viewer "…." (no comments or hearts or response)

New 'scope broadcaster "No really, Guys I have something important to tell you – tell all of your followers to join"

New 'scope viewer "…." (NEW SCOPE VIEWER IS THINKING – I just stumbled upon your broadcast for the first time, I don't know you from Adam, why don't you start dropping value and I'll decide if it's worthy of bugging my whopping 10 Periscope followers about…)

New 'scope broadcaster "Guuuys!!! Really, I need you to…."

New 'scope viewer (New scope viewer is thinking)– "I'm OUT! However, This was a MASSIVE waste of 30 seconds of my time that I cannot recapture and I will be forever …OH look @tomgreenlive!"

-END SCENE-

The moral of the story here is drop VALUE and GREET PEOPLE (or their profiles) before you ever start asking them to do something that will only benefit you.

*BTW @gitomer should be on Periscope (as of now 7/3/15) but, @grantcardone is crushing it in your absence.

Chapter 6 – Mistake #3:

Bad Thumbnails

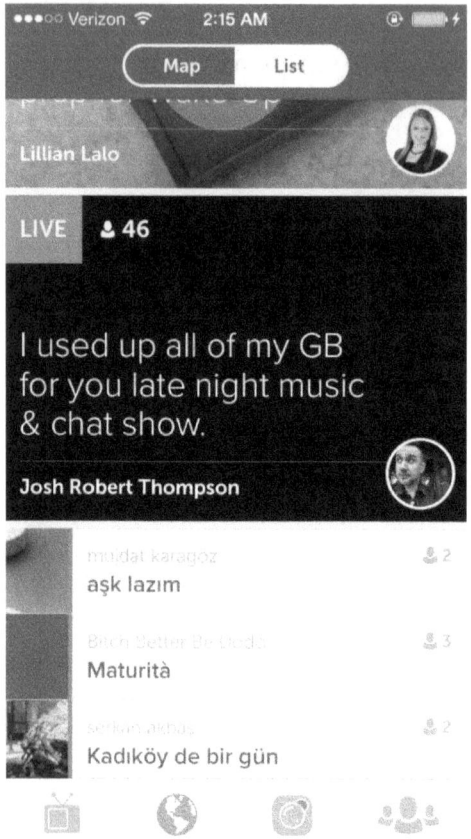

The above pic (with black background) is an example of a bad thumbnail

After the title that you choose – the most important aspect of promoting your broadcast is having a good thumbnail. Many people – when they first sign up for Periscope and begin to broadcast often pay no mind to their thumbnail picture.

There may be a number of reasons why this is ignored but it's a problem that is very easy to fix. Right before you press "START BROADCAST" whatever your back camera is focused on using your phone or mobile device is what will become the thumbnail. SIMPLE.

Oftentimes that camera is pointed at the ground, carpet, jeans or the ceiling with no care. As long as you take care to focus the camera you will stand out amongst the 80 -90% who pay no attention to this aspect.

Chapter 7 – Mistake #4:

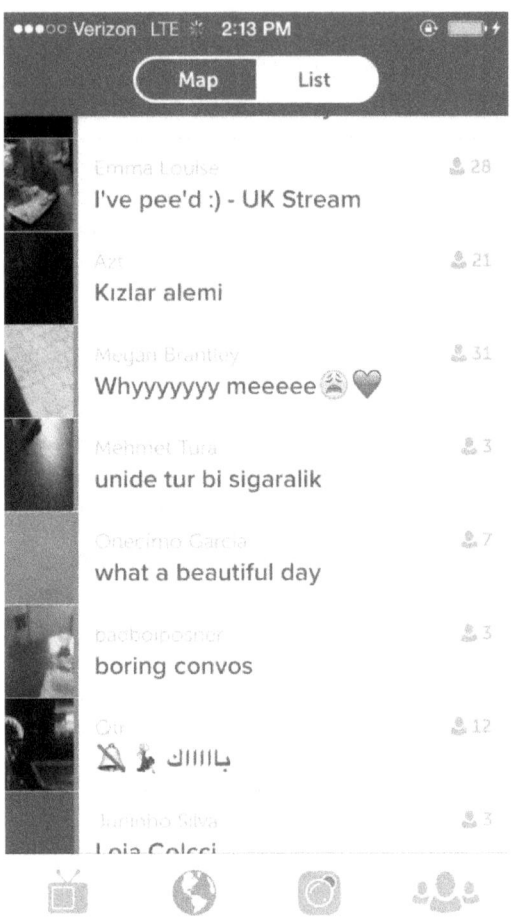

Not using marks or symbols

As mentioned earlier the most important part of your broadcast is your title. This will draw people in repel them depending on the care or lack thereof you give to the title. Since Periscope is used on global basis not everyone viewing your broadcast or deciding whether or not they should join or replay your broadcast will speak your same language. That being said, a mistake some people make is not using Marks and symbols to further describe their broadcast.

There are three types of symbols that you should try to incorporate with your title and those include:

Hashtags (#)

So hashtags are basically placing a "#" before a specific subject or word that your broadcast is about. If you are broadcasting for example a sunset. A title of

"Watching the #sunset in #AZ"

Will likely do better than simply:

"Watching the sunset in AZ"

This is because by putting the "#" in front of word it makes it much easier to search and find for people looking for that specific thing on Twitter and also within the Periscope app itself. When in doubt use hashtags – however don't go overboard 2-3 hashtags in a title is a good amount. Any more than that and your title may become a little too busy.

Emoji's

Not using Emoji's – (aka happy faces, sad faces and pictures , etc) can decrease the number of people who decide to check out your broadcast. Again since Periscope is a global social network – already at it's infancy you could have people who view English as a 2nd language deciding whether or not to view your broadcast.

They may be interested in say a sunset but if their unfamiliar with the word "sunset" and see no other visual clues to entice them they will likely avoid clicking on or checking out your broadcast.

Use of Twitter Handles

Finally using Twitter handles of people or organizations that you are discussing, with or even physically at during your broadcast will help both grab your audience's attention and in turn the attention of their followers which can indirectly shine on you.

So for example if you were at the offices of Carte Blanche Media it would behoove you to use a title like:

"At the offices of @carteblanchme [our Twitter handle] really enjoying our #periscope conversation."

if you put an alternative

"At the offices of Carte Blanche Media enjoying our periscope conversation"

A couple things won't happen.

#1) My company account will not get an automatic notification that I was mentioned

#2) Anyone who is interested in the subject of periscope will likely miss out since the "#" mark was not used.

Chapter 8 – Mistake #5:

No Focus

This is an issue that some early scopers have and shouldn't especially if they are business focused. If you are broadcasting for your business you should not treat your broadcast as a simple community chat time unless it's on a specific subject guided by you.

Instead have an intention with what you would like to accomplish with the broadcast. It could be a number of things.

We'll go over strategies in a later chapter but have a vision of what you would like to accomplish or help your target customer out with before you hit the "START BROADCAST" button.

Section 3:
Techniques to Embrace

As the title suggests, these are techniques to embrace when periscoping. If you follow these techniques you'll get a lot more traction with your periscope broadcasts.

Chapter 9 – Technique #1:

Having a good title

As mentioned in the prior section – having an untitled or poorly titled Periscope broadcast is possibly one of the biggest mistakes that you can make.

Conversely, having a good title is something that will attract new viewers to your broadcast and potentially convince them to peer into your world when they wouldn't before.

As a general rule your title should be one or more of the 3 E's: **Enticing, Entertaining** or **Educational**.

Enticing: Any title you have should be enticing in some way. Obviously this varies wildly depending on who your target market is.

That being said a good rule of thumb to have a title that is enticing is to have some information in the title that hints at being either

Entertaining

or

Educational

So Entertaining titles might be something like:

"How your business will look like once you start using XYZ widgets"

or

"Here is a view from behind the scenes at the biggest widget factory in

North America!"

For a more Educational title you might use something similar to:

"5 tips you need to know to get good at Periscope"

Or

"10 best niche markets for carpet cleaners"

Obviously you can use your imagination depending on your market but the bottom line is that the business periscope broadcasts that get the most attention and likes, Retweets and follows share some sort of value. So be aware of this.

Chapter 10 – Technique #2:

Using Emoji's

As mentioned before, having emoji's in your title will potentially attract audience members who may overlook your broadcast without them. On other social media platforms this may look childish and immature however, due to the inherently visual nature of Periscope Emoji's can make the difference between someone choosing your broadcast or the one directly above or below yours.

This goes back to having a great title to use with your broadcast.

The great thing about Periscope is that there are full sections devoted to different emoji's or pictures once you press the "Emoji" or Happy face icon on your operating system right before you broadcast.

They range in 7 main categories (for illustration purposes I've included pics of the different categories as it shows on a IOS system):

People/Faces

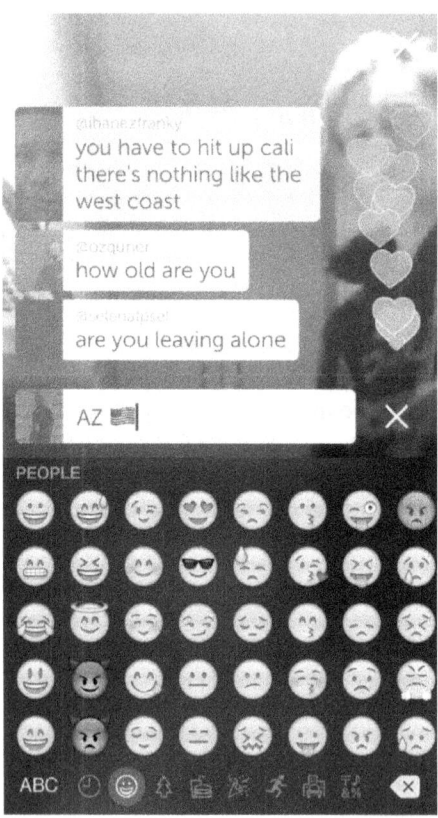

Nature

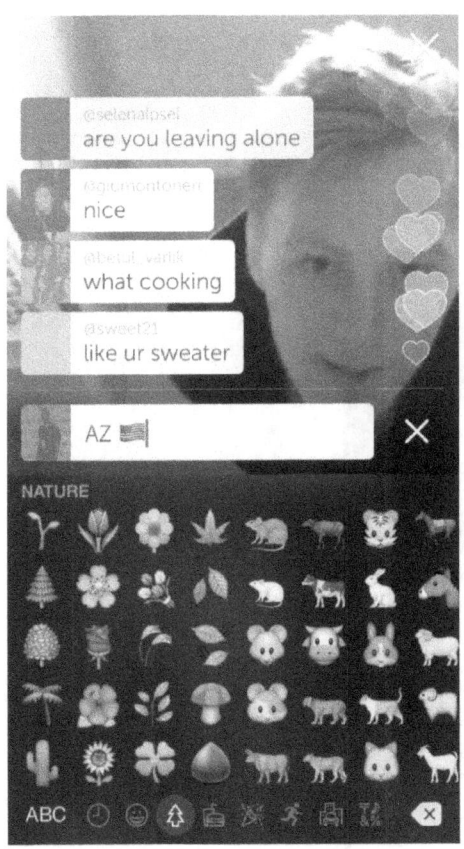

Food & Drink

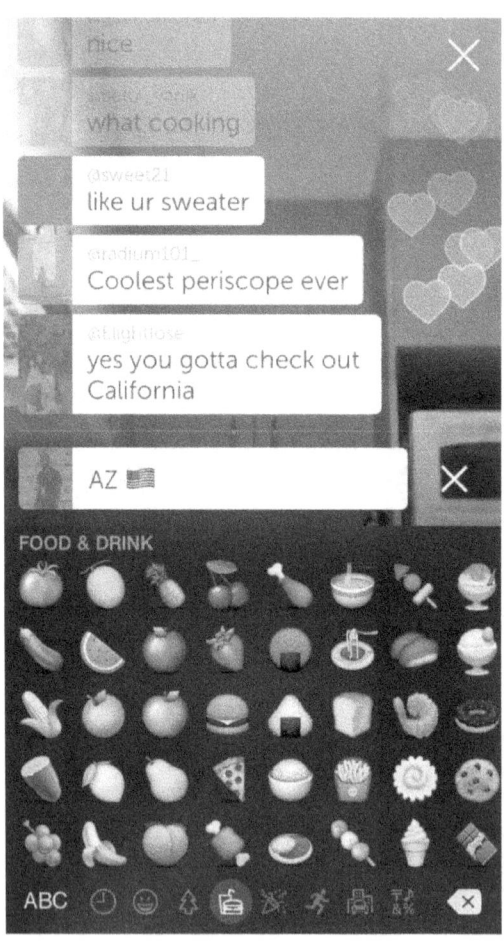

Celebration

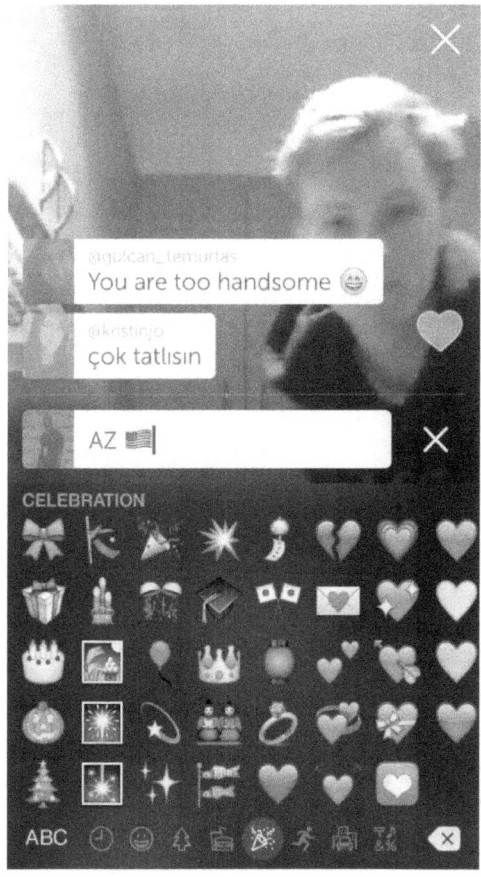

Activity

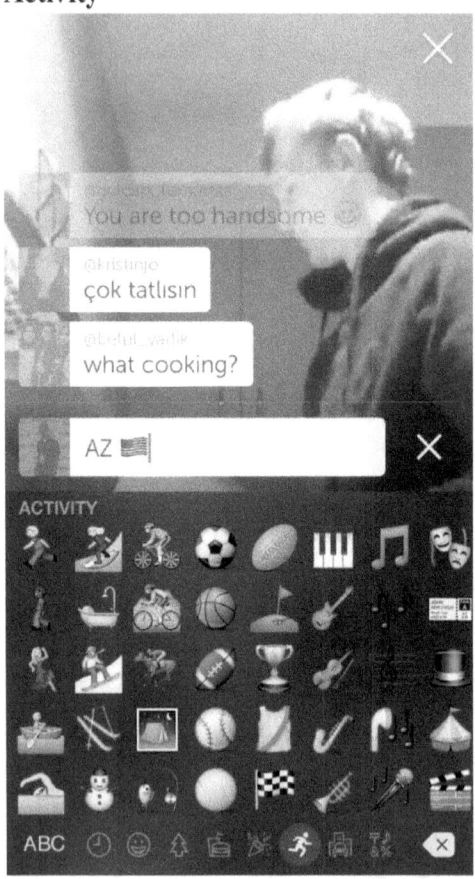

Travel & Places

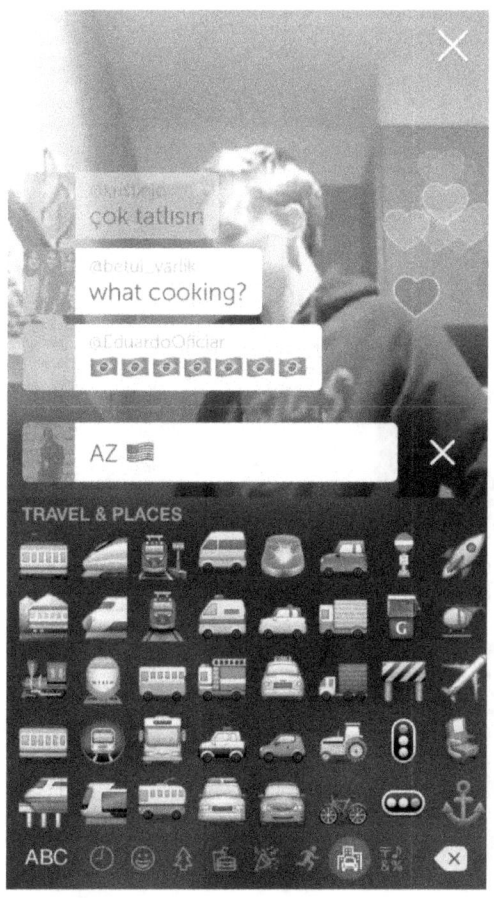

Objects & Symbols

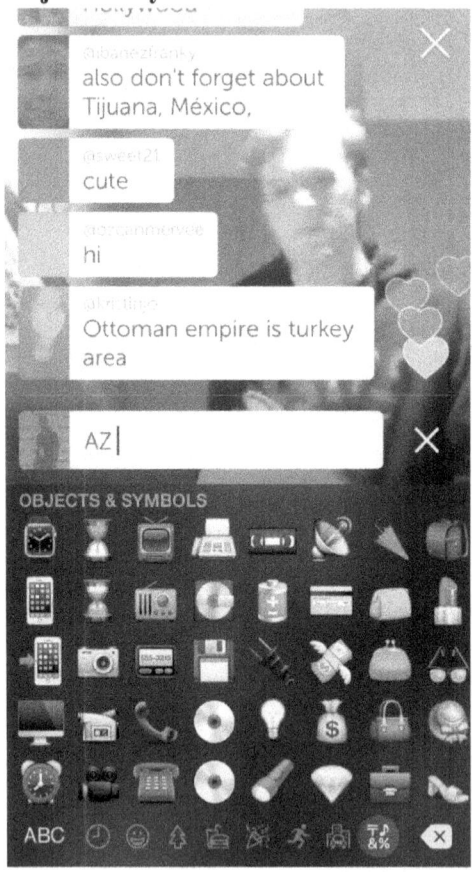

An eighth unofficial category is **Frequently Used** which as the name implies will save the 25-30 or so emoji's you've used most recently. This category will become the first section of **Emoji's** once you begin using them.

Chapter 11 – Technique #3:

Using Hashtags

As mentioned before using hashtags is necessary to stand out and also to allow people to find you easier depending on what subject you highlight in your hashtags.

When you use the Hashtag

"#Marketing" anyone who is searching for the term marketing will find your post a little quicker than if you posted the title without a hashtag.

You can also use hashtags if you decide to share another's broadcast while you use it.

Additionally if you are able to get in early enough to a widely watched Periscope broadcast you can use the hashtags to convey the most important part of your message as comments zip by in very active broadcasts.

Chapter 12 – Technique #4:

Using Twitter Handles in Title

If you're addressing an individual or a company with a rather large Twitter following then you should definitely attempt to use the profiles Twitter handle in your title.

This will immediately notify the person or the company's social media team the next time you log in that you mentioned their Twitter handle.

If they are one of many companies that hasn't yet experimented with Periscope they may pay even more attention to you once you bring to the app to their attention and the fact that you mentioned them in your broadcast.

Chapter 13 – Technique #5:

Entertain Your Audience

Your audience or **avatar** in the world of internet Marketing, is shorthand for your "target market" or what an average person from your target market looks like.

As I mentioned earlier a good way to grow an audience or become more in tune with the audience you already possess is to entice them. One of the two best ways to entice them by entertaining them.

Since Periscope is another social media platform it is important that you treat it as such and don't simply use the platform to read off press releases with each post. A more interesting idea is to have fun and or entertain your audience.

You can do this a number of ways some of which we'll go over in the strategy section. Obviously you know your target and you should know what they like and don't like. That being said, the platform is great for testing things out in a way that can either confirm your avatars preferences or show that your assumptions about your target market are wrong.

Chapter 14 – Technique #6:

Educating your avatar

Another technique to embrace is to educate your avatar.

Let's assume for a moment you are a realtor and let's say your avatar is for example – 1st time home Buyers – if you can give basic information on the buying process through Periscope – many of those individuals will be grateful for your contribution and will likely keep you in mind when it's time to purchase a home.

Furthermore, if there is an area that your avatar typically needs help with or has difficulty with and you can ease their pain in some way – they will embrace you even more when it's time to relieve that pain.

Section 4:
Strategies for Business

In this section we'll explore different specific strategies you can use to get more attention and ideally more business by using your periscope account.

Chapter 15 - Tips & Tricks

One strategy to begin to bring people into your funnel and attract them to your product or service is to offer tips and tricks they can use. By doing this you'll accomplish a couple things.

1) You'll bring value to the table
2) If you bring enough value people will recommend you to others who will likely also be within your avatar/target market

3) You will position yourself and/or your company as experts in the field and thus make it easier for your avatar to justify buying from you.

Chapter 16 – Behind the Scenes

This is a very nice way to build on any brand loyalty you may have already obtained. People are constantly curious about aspects of life or other people's lives that they do not get to see. If you show them behind the scenes footage – they will become instantly engaged and make them feel loyal to you in a way competitors won't be able to share unless they begin to Periscope as well.

3 great examples of this would be

1) @kevinolearytv – the "Mr. Wonderful" of the ABC business show Shark Tank. Mr. O'leary did a Periscope in between shoots for the acclaimed TV show today.

2) @thesharkdaymond – Daymond John of the same show was competing with his boardroom rival to see who could get more viewers at the same time.

3) @Lizkotalik – finally Liz Kotalik is a Tuscon, AZ area news broadcaster who was one of the first TV broadcasters to begin doing consistent Periscope broadcasts from her phone. She currently has about 5 million hearts and they continue to grow whenever she broadcasts. She has her phone set to her side and in between broadcasts she chat with her audience using the tool.

Chapter 17 - Following Thought leaders

Following thought leaders in your industry is a good strategy to not only learn from them but also to be able to communicate with them when they decide to broadcast.

A good example of this is one very popular and very active Broadcaster by the name of Grant Cardone (@grantcardone). Grant Cardone is a sales expert, based out of Miami who regularly has 300+ people begin to view his broadcasts within moments of him beginning a broadcast.

People who are also in the sales training industry and want to learn from one of the most popular broadcasters can model their scopes after his without completely copying everything he does.

Likewise – if you and the thought leader are after the same type of avatar you can potentially offer assistance to others who were blocked out of commenting during a broadcast and/or cannot quite yet afford to pay for the thought leaders services but can make a budget for your current rate.

Obviously the goal is not outright steal clients from big name competitors but by being helpful or even disagreeing with a thought leader you may offer yourself as an alternative to what other potential clients either can't afford or are turned off by due to a thought leaders habits or views.

Another example is someone who is well known within another industry but gets an instant reaction either in a positive or negative direction due to his personality and also his use of profanity. If you're the squeaky clean alternative or the brash and edgy alternate option people will be attracted to you based on their own personal preferences and ideals.

Chapter 18 – Use of Hashtags

This is a great way to find like-minded people instantly online and show them value without even broadcasting. Typically as a broadcaster's audience grows the Periscope app will begin to limit the ability of people to comment depending on how interactive their audience is.

That being said, if you are one of the first 100-200 people on a broadcast you typically are given the ability to comment on the broadcast.

You can select other viewers directly to respond to by tapping on their comments as they travel up your screen and then choosing the "reply" option as they are talking.

You can learn a lot of things about other viewers based both on their comments, their bio and even their Periscope handle can give you indications that this profile is an average avatar for you or outside of your target market to begin with.

Chapter 19 - Tweet while watching

Another great feature that was just added in June of 2015 is the "Share on Twitter" option which allows you to post the fact that you are watching an interesting broadcast as you watch it.

This can be a great way to promote your business and reinforce your branding depending on what you watch and what you add as your comment to your viewing.

Chapter 20 - CTA during Broadcasts

Any long term marketer knows that **CTA** stands for "**Call to Action**". The problem is that few people always use the CTA in their broadcasts even if they're in business. This is tricky problem because if you do use a CTA during every broadcast or worst multiple times during a broadcast you may very well turn off viewers and they will never want to watch your broadcast ever again.

For those more familiar with business functions other than marketing some good examples of a CTA on periscope would be:

-Tap your screen/Give me hearts
-Follow me
-Go to my website
-Buy my book
-Join my course
-Give me your email
-etc.

The flip side is that you NEVER use a CTA during your broadcast – then what is the point of having Periscope account for business anyway? You might as well just have a personal account.

The best rule of thumb is to attempt to achieve a happy medium of giving value and then more value and more value and then as an afterthought – asking – or trying to sell your audience on the CTA.

This advice is not new and has been given in multiple places before – most notably by Bob Burg and John David Mann authors of the book "The Go-Giver" and by Gary Vaynerchuk – the author of "Jab, Jab, Jab – Right Hook". Both books go over the same concept.

So what are good rules of thumb?

In this regard I would say to make your CTA's as close to gentle half-hearted thoughts as possible compared to direct orders or commands from a drill sergeant.

During one of my first days on Periscope a broadcaster – who is to my knowledge not well known now – barked at her screen:

"Guys invite your followers now I have something to tell you"

When no one obliged her she only raised her voice louder and repeated the request again. As a result multiple people begin to leave her broadcast, yours truly included.

A better way might've been for her to give value first, see that people are engaged and then say half-heatedly – "Thanks for the hearts guys, hey if you like what I'm saying go ahead and invite your followers and see if they'll enjoy it too"

Chapter 21 – Contests

Contests can be a great way to either gain followers or further engage those who are already following you. If you give away a t-shirt a mug or even digital gifts such as a followback for your users taking action you can gain a lot of interest in a short period of time.

Many times on Periscope the currency is "hearts" since the more hearts a person has the higher up the leaderboard they go and the higher up that board you are, the more exposure you will get.

Although I have never ran a contest myself what I've seen work is as follows:

If you have a large number of followers – you likely don't need to put the word contest in the title just mention it a few times while you're broadcasting.

What Alex Pettit one of the "Most loved" broadcasters typically does is simply says "At the end of this broadcast – whoever has given the most hearts will get a follow back from me"

If you only have a handful of followers you may need to offer something more substantial in order to get people to watch much less "Heart" your broadcast.

Ideas may include a free service, product, T-shirt – etc you can be creative.

Chapter 22 – #Tribes

As I write this, almost ridiculously, within 6 months of the official launch of Periscope, the app itself has gone through an evolutionary journey. From an app with only a few functions and a couple million users to an app that now has in excess of 10 million downloads and so many cool functions and tools to it.

One thing that has been around since around July 2015 but really began to explode in August of 2015 is #tribes or Hashtag Tribes for those unfamiliar with the Twitter nomenclature.

These are groups of Periscoper's who collaborate and support each other in a very organized way. The first of those tribes I recall seeing is the #perigirls – basically any Periscoper who was born with an X chromosome and would like support from her sisters.

However, in August 2015 - the number of #Tribes began to expand dramatically with the introduction of:

#BoPO – a Body Positivity Tribe
#perifamily – Ryan Bell's – founder of PeriscopeSummit
#Tagtribes – the biggest community started by Mark Shaw
#Perigirls – The biggest female only tribe
#Peridudes – A new tribe founded by Kama – the "Spam"(?) Portion of the "Spam" and Rice Periscoping duo

Around mid-august 2015 I noticed people using multiple

"tribe" hashtags begin to subside but who knows if it's just a temporary thing before it begins to increase again.

Section 5:

Genres of 'Scopers

In this section I'll cover some of the different types of Periscoping genres that have occurred since the platform got off the ground nearly 6 months ago. It used to be a mix of people showing little tidbits of their day and those teaching others how to use the platform. The platform has expanded a bit beyond that at this point and although this is by no means an exhaustive list it's a good generalization of some of the main scopes I see out there today.

Chapter 23 – Business 'Scopers

As the name suggests these are people who do most of their scoping on business related topics. Many times the topic is How to Use Periscope for Business. How convenient.

@Alexpettitt

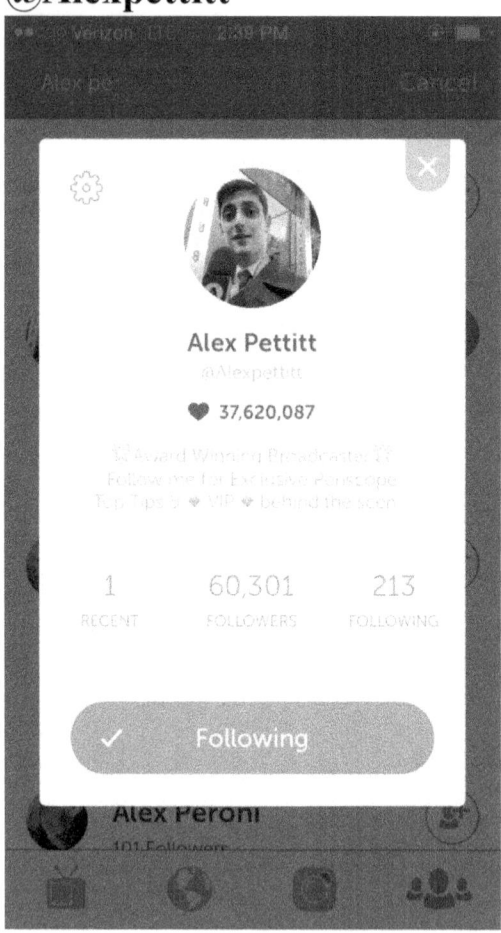

Alex is a 20-something, London-based Periscoper who had around 1,000 Twitter followers (maybe even less than that) around the time that the platform was launched but has since grown his Periscope following to about ~~60,000~~ 165,000 at the time of this writing.

His Twitter following stands at about ~~1,600~~ 5,000 people currently.

Not sure how he did it but Alex apparently learned how to get followers fast on Periscope and apparently knows many of the people who actually run the Periscope app currently – so he's privy to updates that others might not be aware of.

One great thing about Alex is that he always gives value. And he is extremely knowledgeable about the platform.

@Markshaw

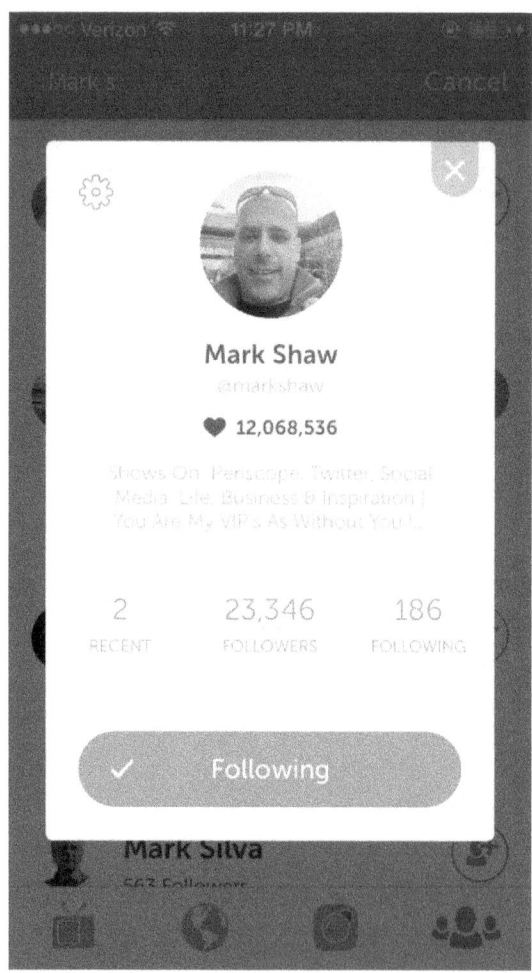

Mark Shaw is another Londoner – possibly a wee bit older than Alex Pettit. Mark focuses on tips and tricks as well with his audience.

That being said he also has a tendency to get a little upset when he sees examples of bad periscoping going on. One example is a broadcast on @therealdonaldtrump and @HillaryClinton who both did poor initial periscopes according to Mr. Shaw.

One thing is for sure though both of these boys (men) from Great Britain do excellent jobs keeping their audiences informed and entertained and this is why they are both very close to the top of the "MOST LOVED" section of periscope.

Update: Mark is also the proud owner/founder of (last I checked) the largest tribe on Periscope #tagtribes.

@RobertCStern

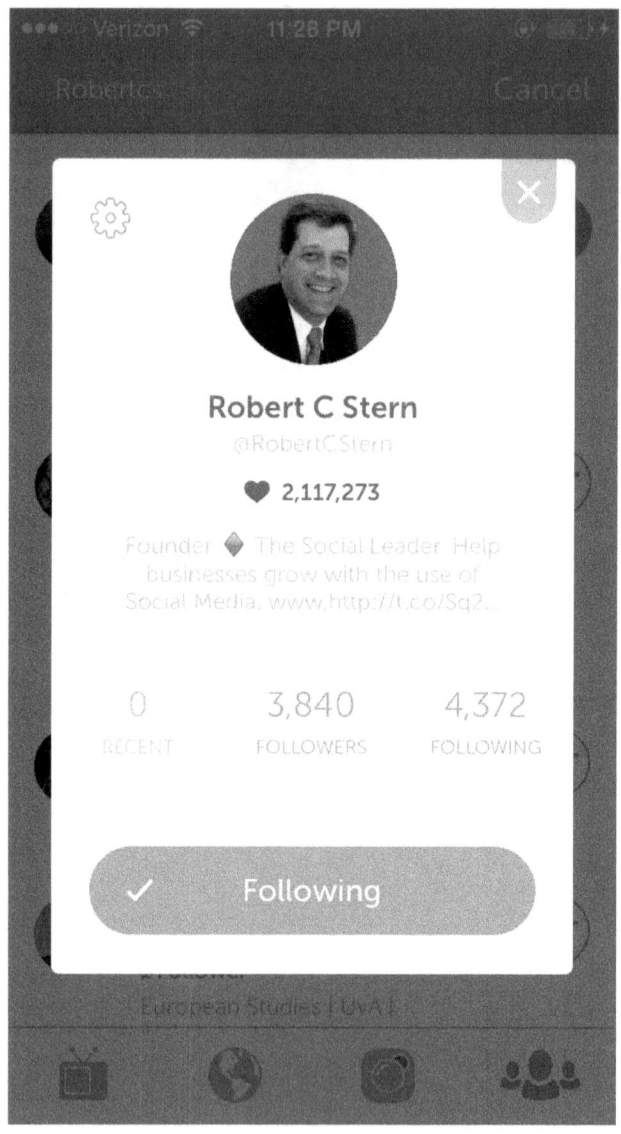

Robert Stern is a social media guy from New Jersey and he runs another social media company – The Social Leader. Robert also tends to give out tips and tricks at day and mixes it with entertaining sidebars performed by both him and his daughter – typically at night.

Robert is always super friendly with his viewers and takes the time to get to know them and build relationships as he goes.

One key difference between Robert and other broadcasters is that he does not outright ask for hearts for the information and value he gives.

NEW: Robert Stern has now developed a healthy(?) Blab addiction so you may find him on that platform a decent amount as well. In fact for a while (maybe a week or two) he held the record for longest continuous blab – but that's another story for another book.

@RyanSteinolfson

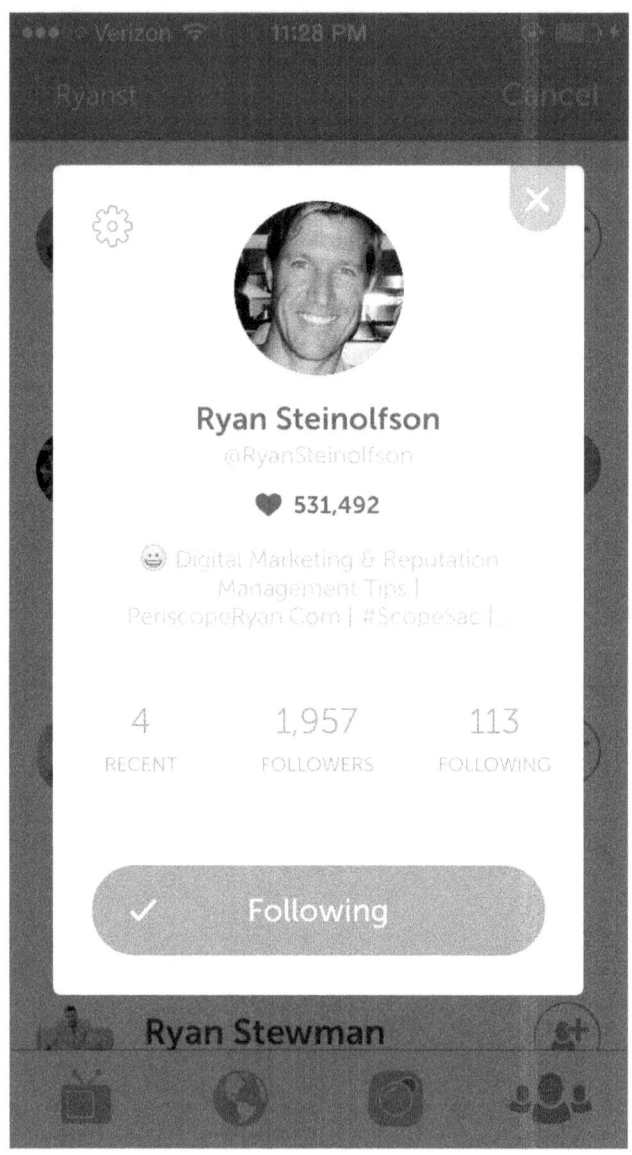

Ryan Steinolfson is also a great business broadcaster but he tends to niche his broadcasts to speak more to avid periscopers and focuses a lot on higher level gear and add-ons for those who are already fairly advanced with their Periscoping skills.

Previous broadcasts have been on everything from How to make your Twitter broadcasts post directly to Facebook to how to save the broadcasts including hearts and comments to YouTube.

He definitely is the more techy of the business scopers however, he is a complete California guy – typically wearing his hat and shorts – that splits part of his time in Florida as well.

@Cathyhackl

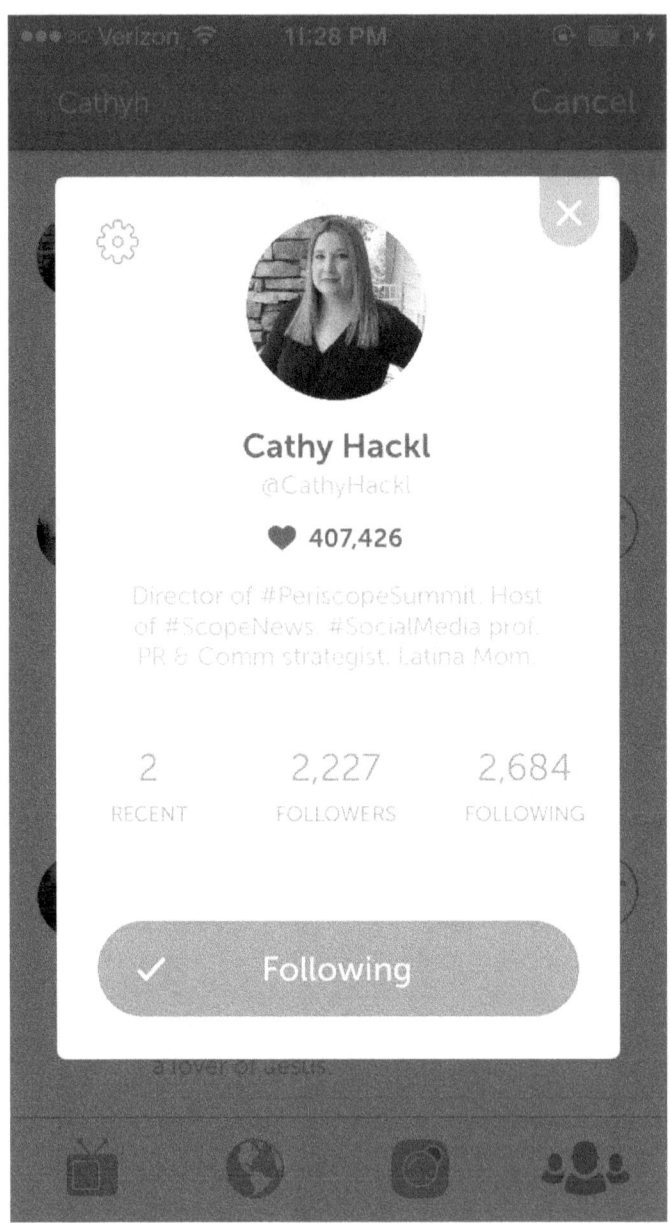

Cathy is one of the most loved female business scopers. In addition to being a female businesswoman – she also is the PR director for Periscope Summit – a Periscope user event being planned currently – she is also a bilingual Latina thus she is something in the realm of triple or quadruple threat.

Chapter 24 – Tourscopers

As the name implies, these are periscopers who share their cities and countries with the world by Periscoping about them.

@Clairewad (Paris). –

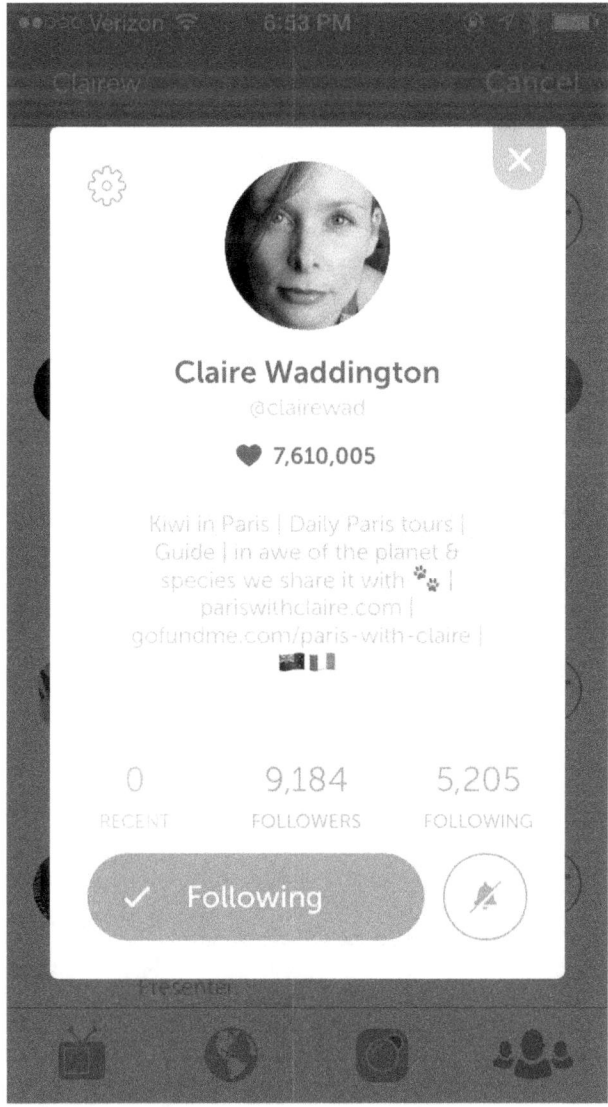

Claire Waddington is a New Zealander who happens to reside in Paris. She also happens to be a tour guide and thus you - as a person who speaks English as your first language- ends up winning.

She tours all of the wonderful sights of Paris including but not limited to the Eiffel tower, The Louvre and can be often found on or around the Seine river.

@GIULIOBASE (Italy) –

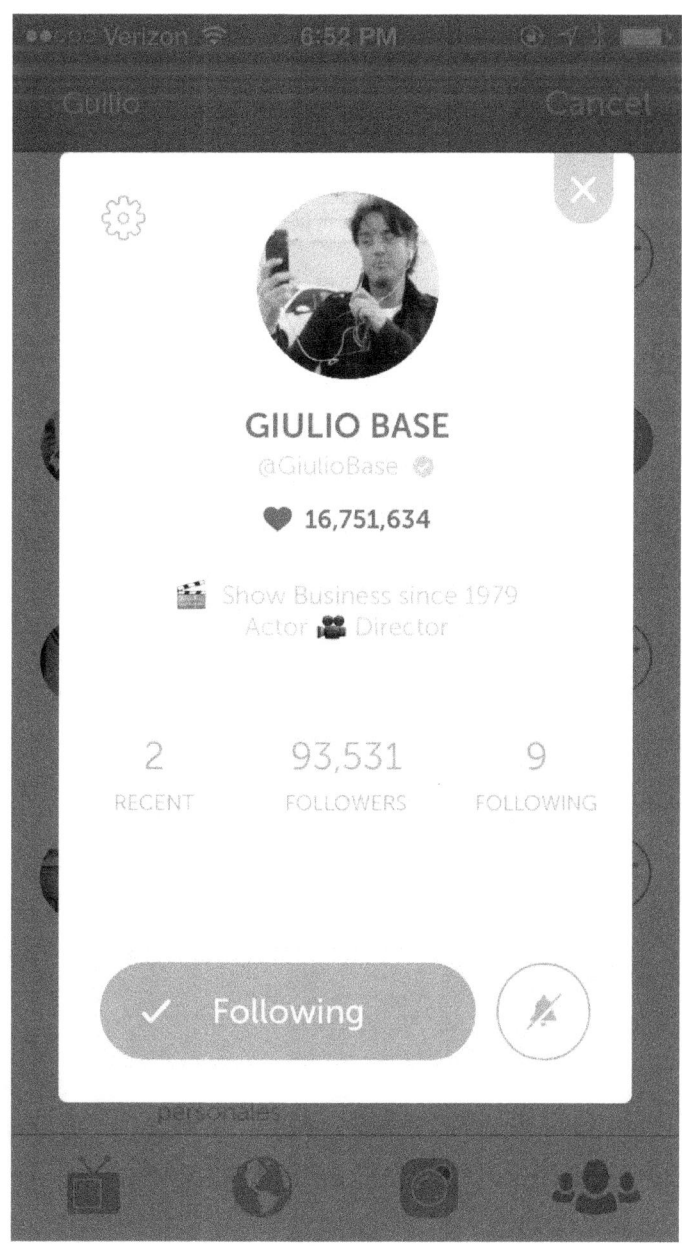

Giulio Base is an Italian with great English skills who takes daily tours of Italy – often with his family in tow.

Lately he's been exploring the beach on various Italian and European coasts. But in the past I've witnessed fantastic tours of Rome and Milan.

@MOEINTERACTIVE (NYC) –

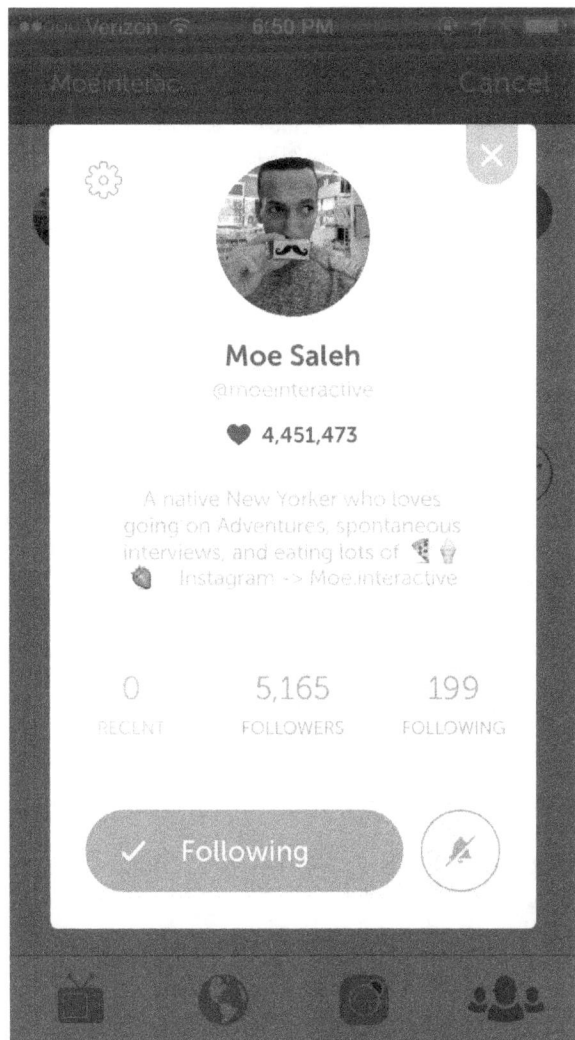

Moe is a New York City based Periscoper and gives virtual tours to those who have never been and those who have been away for a while – showing his audience what's going on in the city that never sleeps.

@EuroMaestro (Paris/Europe) –

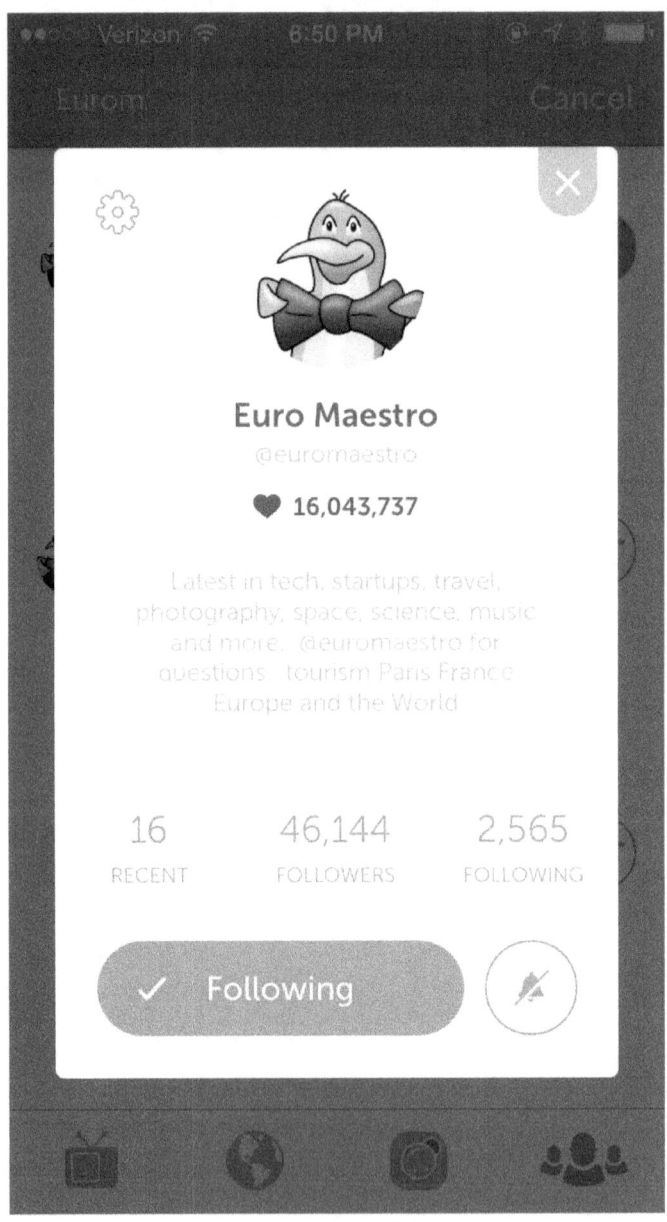

Euro Maestro is a tech geek –with an American or maybe North American accent – who is based out of Europe. He rarely [if ever] shows his face but always does pretty exciting scopes.

In August of 2015 he and a few other well known periscopers were invited to Dubai and he Periscoped their experience there.

@penguinsix (Hong Kong) -

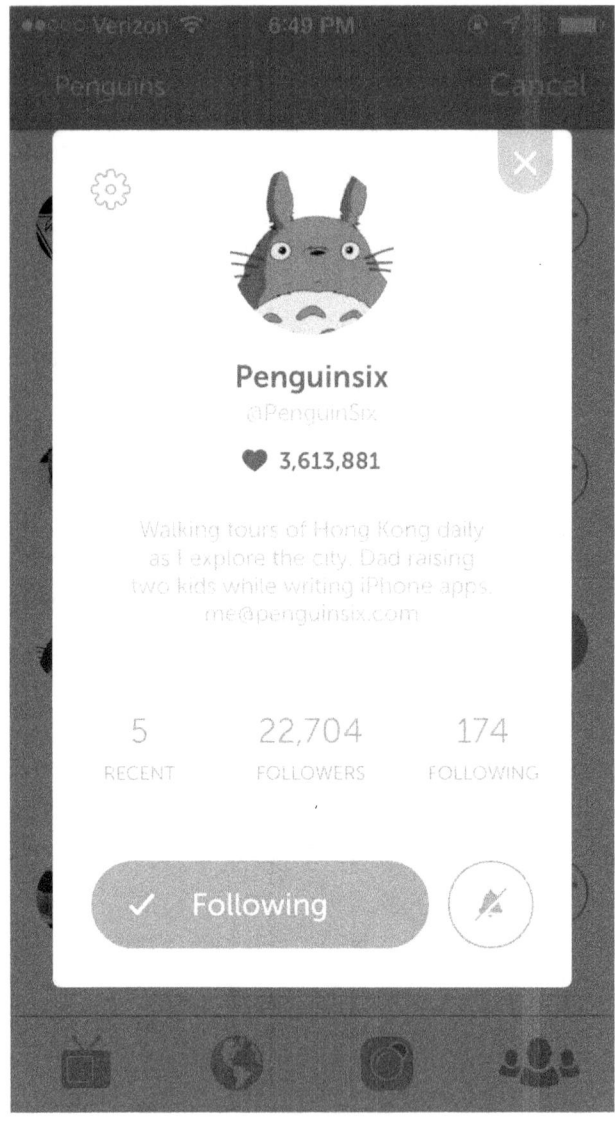

Is an American living in Hong Kong who does

wonderful periscopes of all things Hong Kong on a daily basis.

On the most recent one I was able to catch he did a fantastic scope from Victoria's peak – the highest peak in Hong Kong that looks down on the city. The view was/is tremendous.

@kanji_k (Osaka, Japan) –

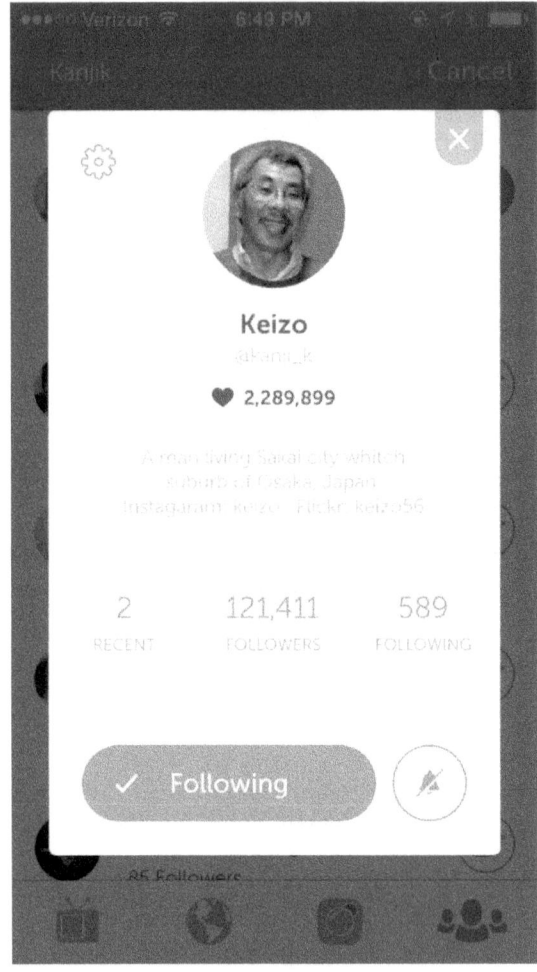

is a Japanese native who speaks English and gives tours of Osaka mainly but I believe I've caught him navigating to other parts of Japan as well.

Chapter 25 – Comedians

Since I'm not funny at all – at least not intentionally – I'll save the attempts at humor and say that these people are comedians and thus much funnier than me and potentially you depending on the night of your set.

@JasonStolken –

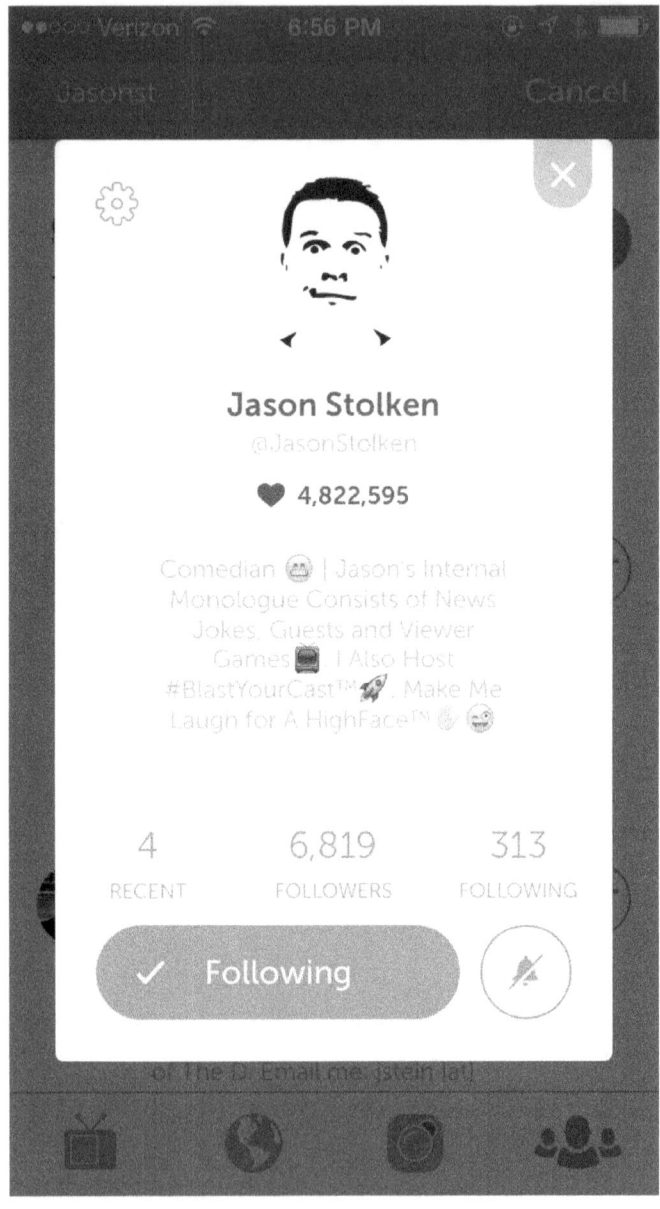

Definitely one of the earliest comedians to jump on to

Periscope. He typically hosts a scope where people can come in and network with one another on what they do and what they scope about.

@BradmanTV –

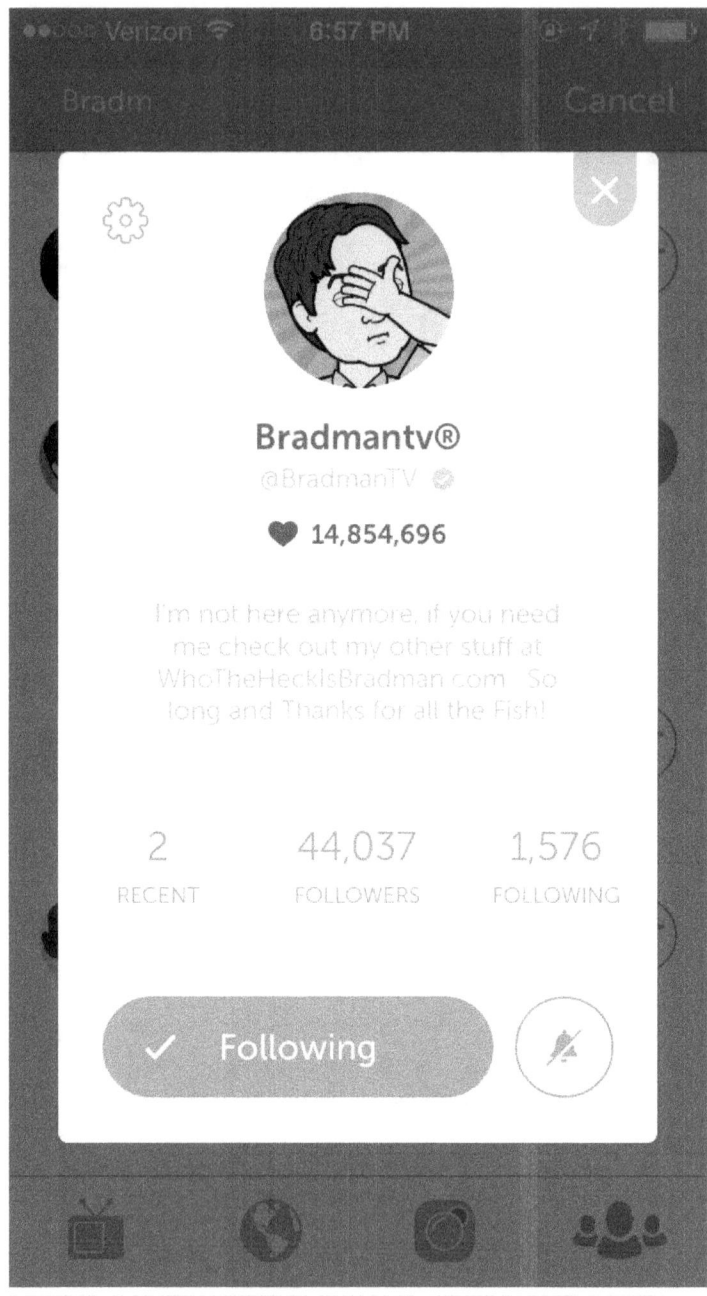

For a long time Bradman was one of the top Periscopers – along with Amanda Oleander but he was surpassed in the last few months as more and more people with large Twitter following joined the platform.

If you read his bio currently – I think that says about his approach with the platform currently. #former lifescoper.

@markkayeshow –

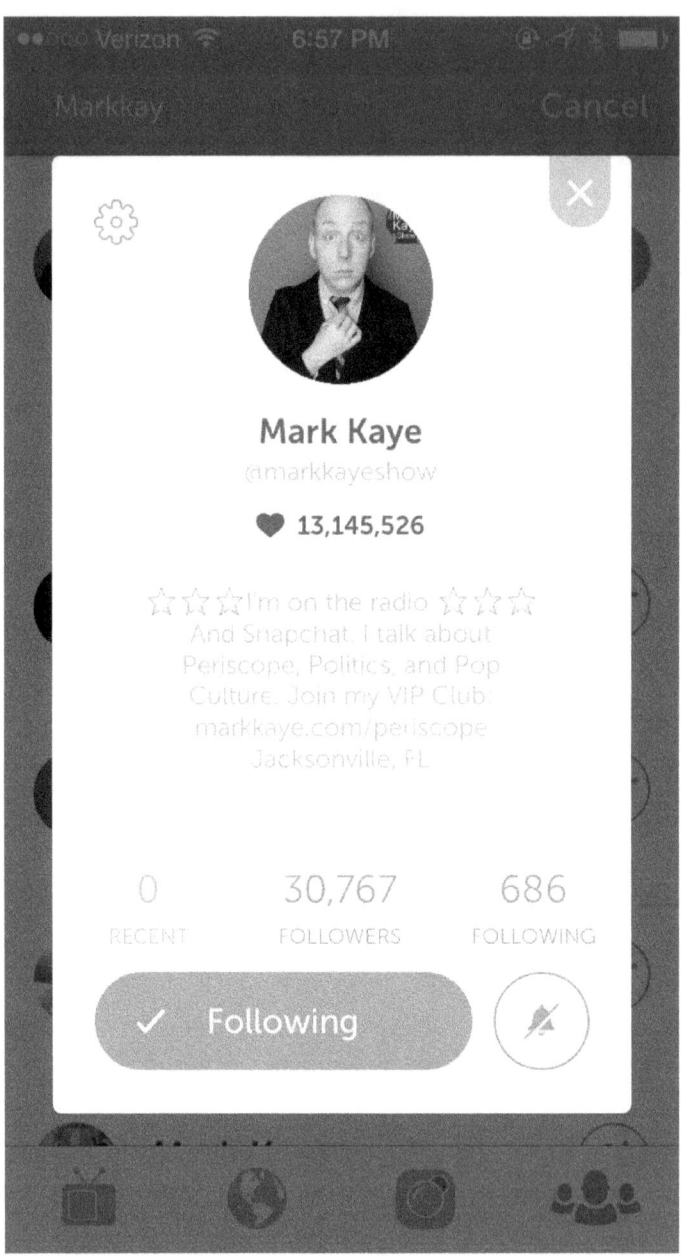

One of the more loved comedians on Periscope. He was also a co-host/M.C. for many of the events that went on during Periscope Summit – which I had the pleasure of attending.

@andydick –

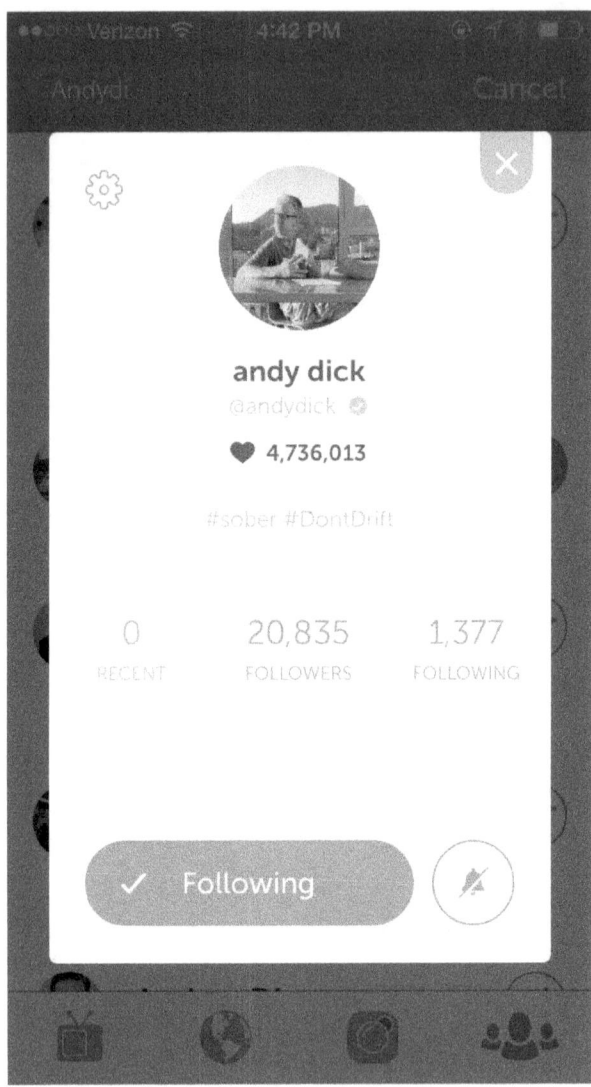

You may have heard of Andy Dick. Recovering drug addict – some-would-say a little bit strange. He periscopes on a fairly regular basis.

@tomgreenlive [Tom Green]–

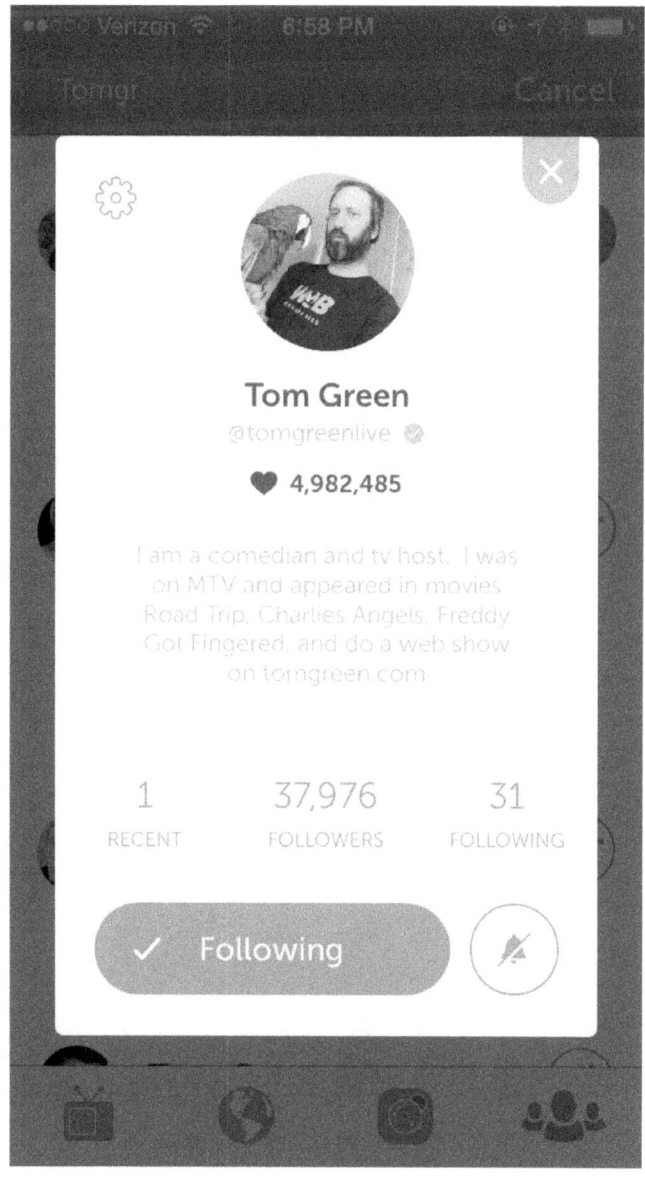

If you are a child of the 80's you may remember Tom Green from your teens – like I do – Tom Green had his own show on MTV for a period and was one of the first Comedians to embrace Periscope.

@SandyChoiRadio [Sandy Choi] –

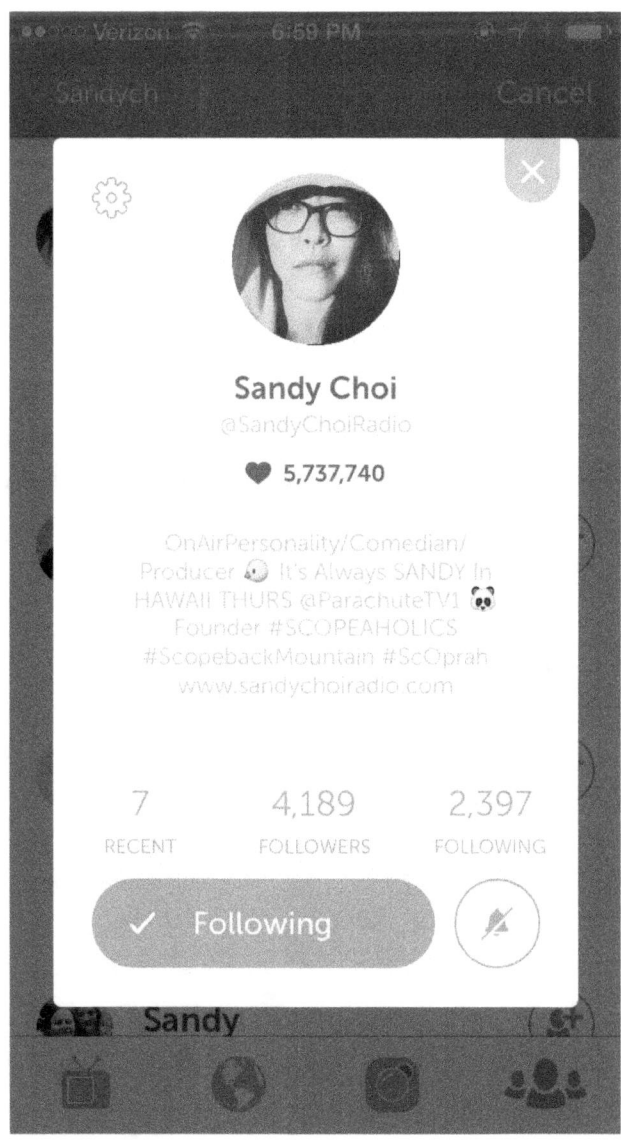

Is a Hawaiian radio host and comedian who has

accumulated quite a following on Periscope . She also hosts a Scopeaholics broadcast on a fairly regular basis.

Chapter 26 – NEWSCASTERS

@LizKotalik – [Liz Kotalik]

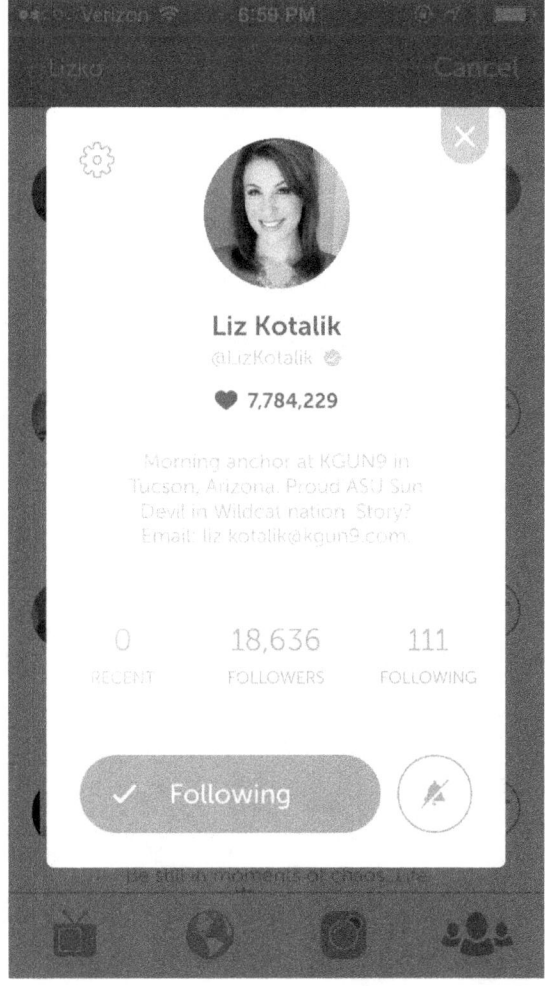

Was the first newscaster, that I know of, to really get into Periscoping. She is a morning news anchor – at this moment – based out of Tuscon, AZ. She typically does behind the scenes broadcasting and talks to her audience in between newscasts.

@scottbudman [Scott Budman] –

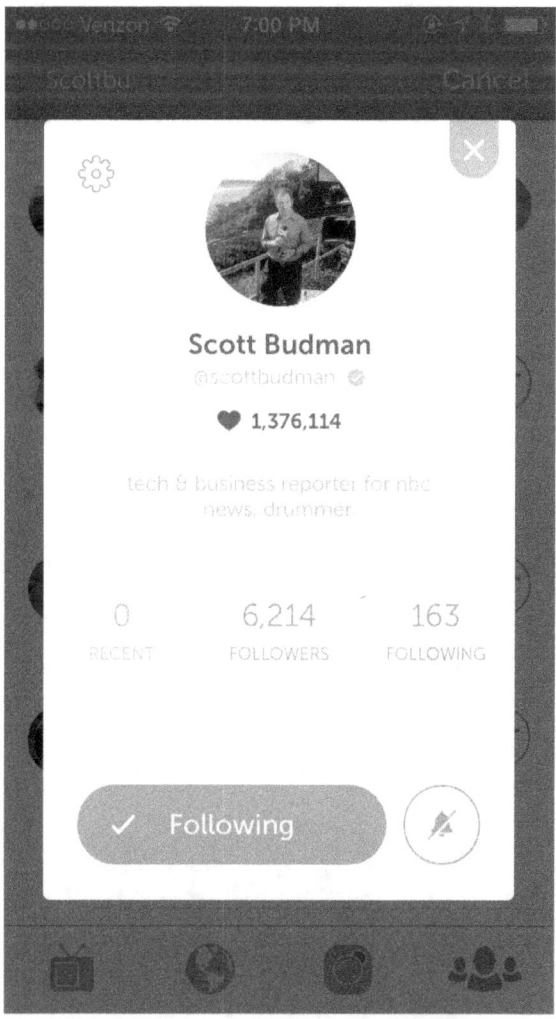

Is a tech reporter for NBC. Since he is based out of Silicon Valley he typically has the scoop on a lot of tech news coming out of the most advanced tech-savvy valley in America.

@Stone_SkyNews [Mark Stone]–

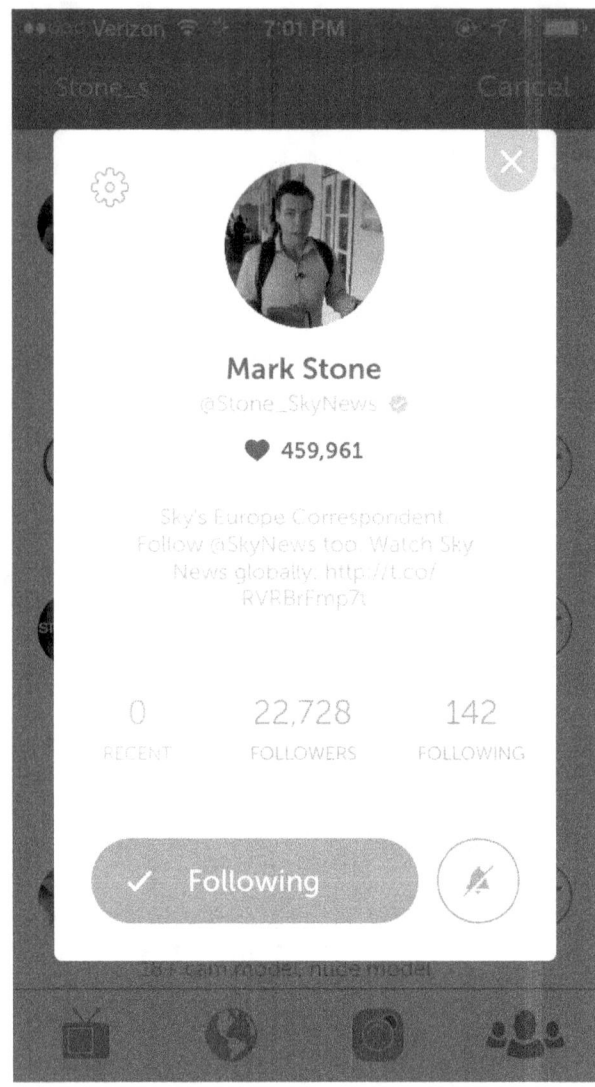

Mark Stone is a reporter for the UK's Sky news. He keeps the periscope world up to date on what's going on in Europe and more specifically the British isles.

@JackSmithIV –Jack Smith –

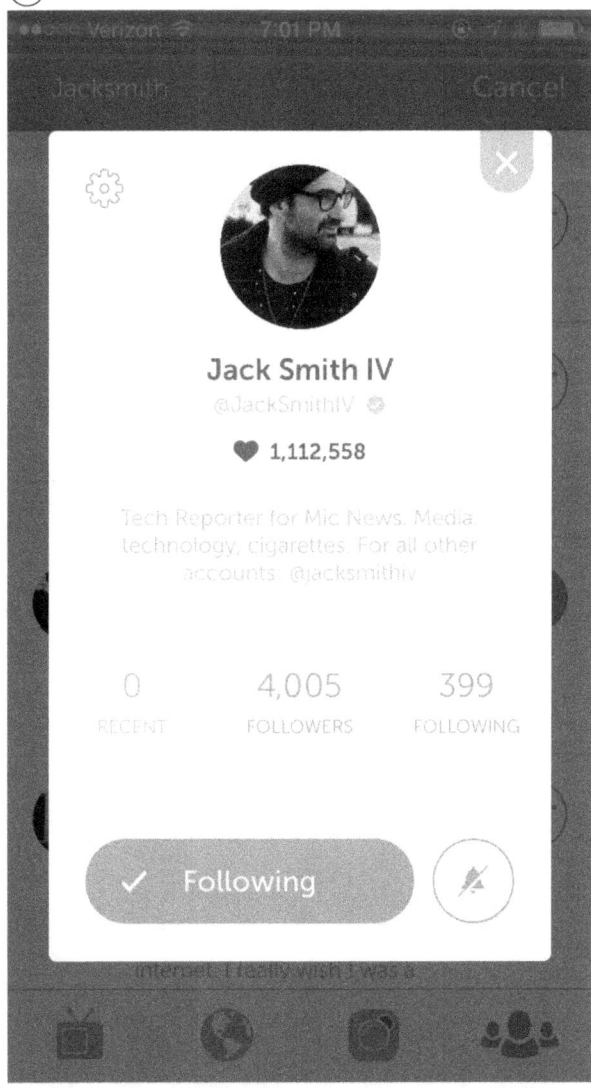

Jack Smith is another tech reporter who has grown quite a following on Periscope. Jack is based out of NYC so he has some of the best news coming out of the east coast.

Chapter 27 – Motivators

As the title implies these are people who definitely offer some motivation on a regular basis.

@1justice4all – Justice Bowens

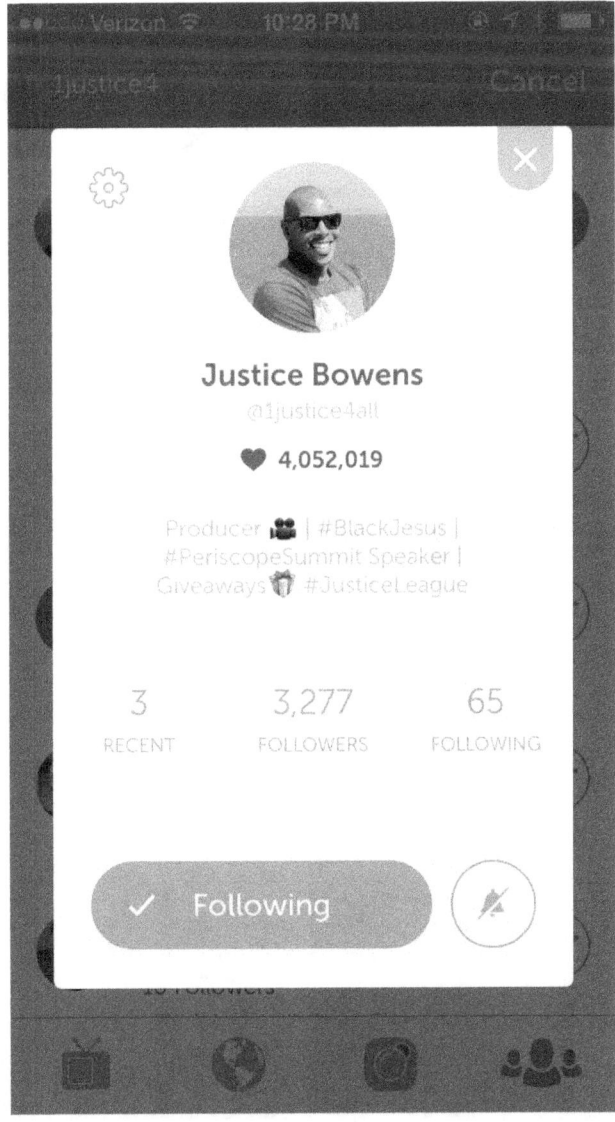

Justice Bowens is an actor, producer and father based out of L.A. He does a twice daily motivational periscope during the weekdays.

@ScottWilliams –

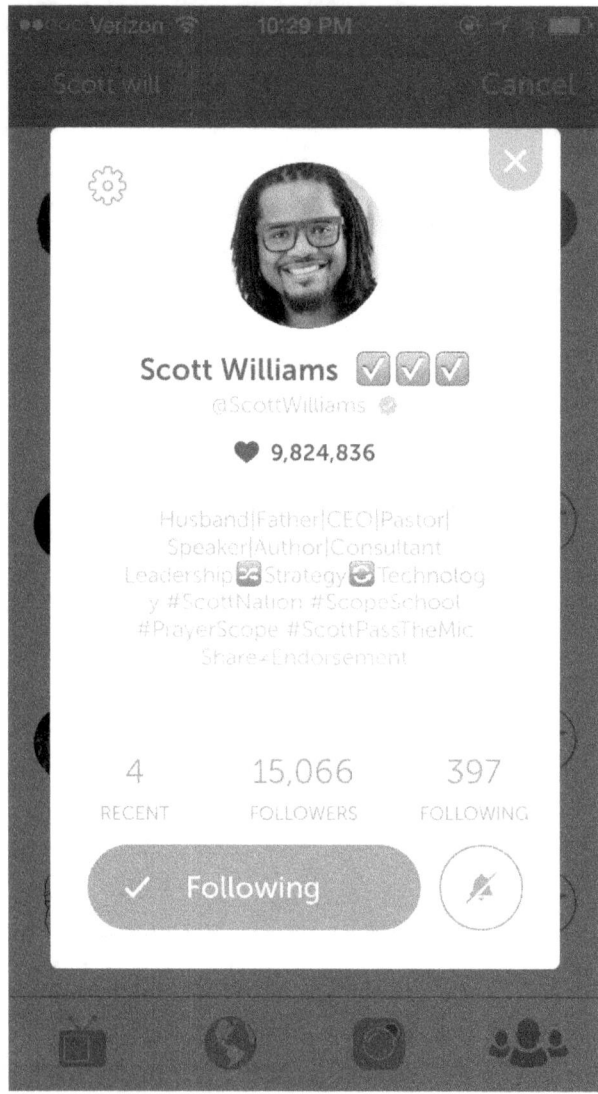

Scott Williams Is a Pastor and Motivator based out of Oklahoma City, OK.

c_ @xoxoLizza –

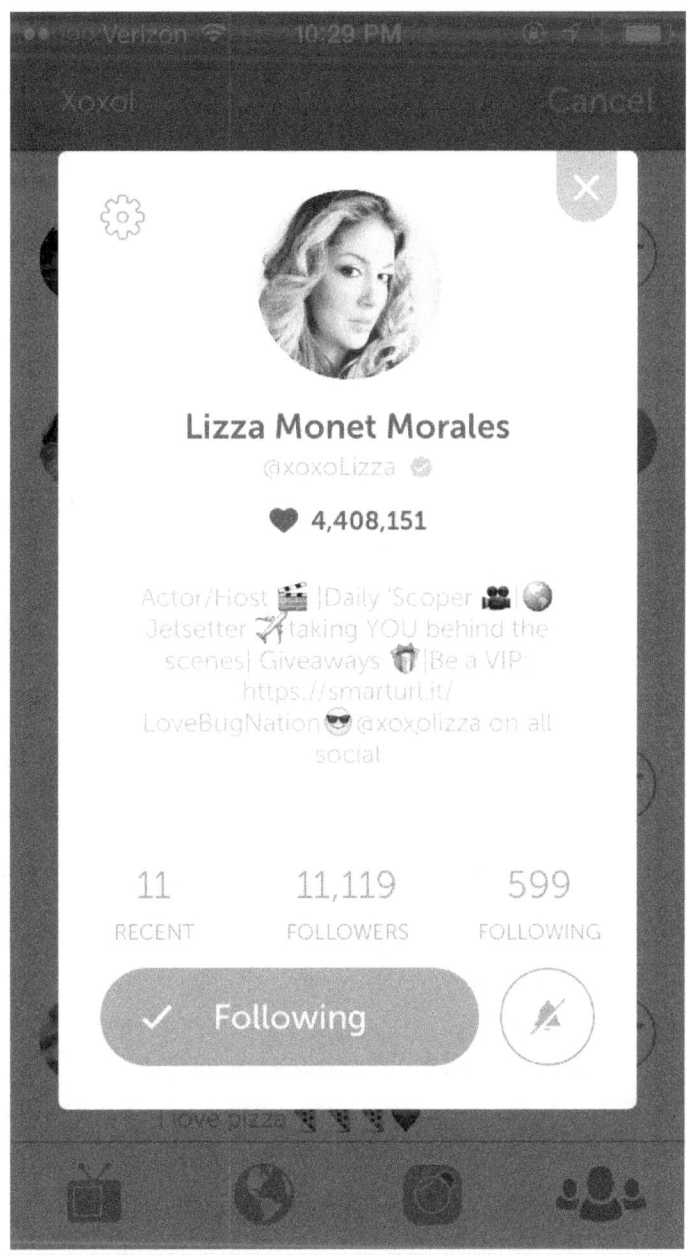

Lizza is a very entertaining Social Media Maven with lots (50k+) of
followers on Twitter.

d_ @1AlexKhan – Alex Khan

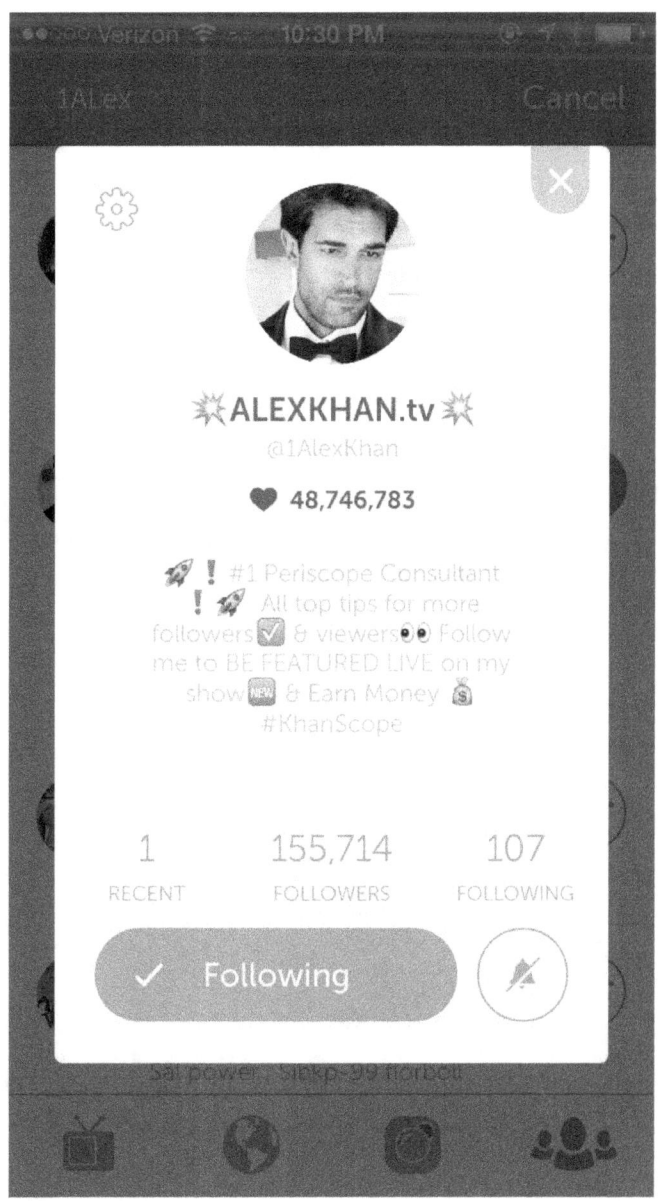

Is a male model with a very Schwarzenegger – esque accent… gives out motivation and Periscope tips regularly.

e_ @Misscleveland1 – Charissa Cleveland -

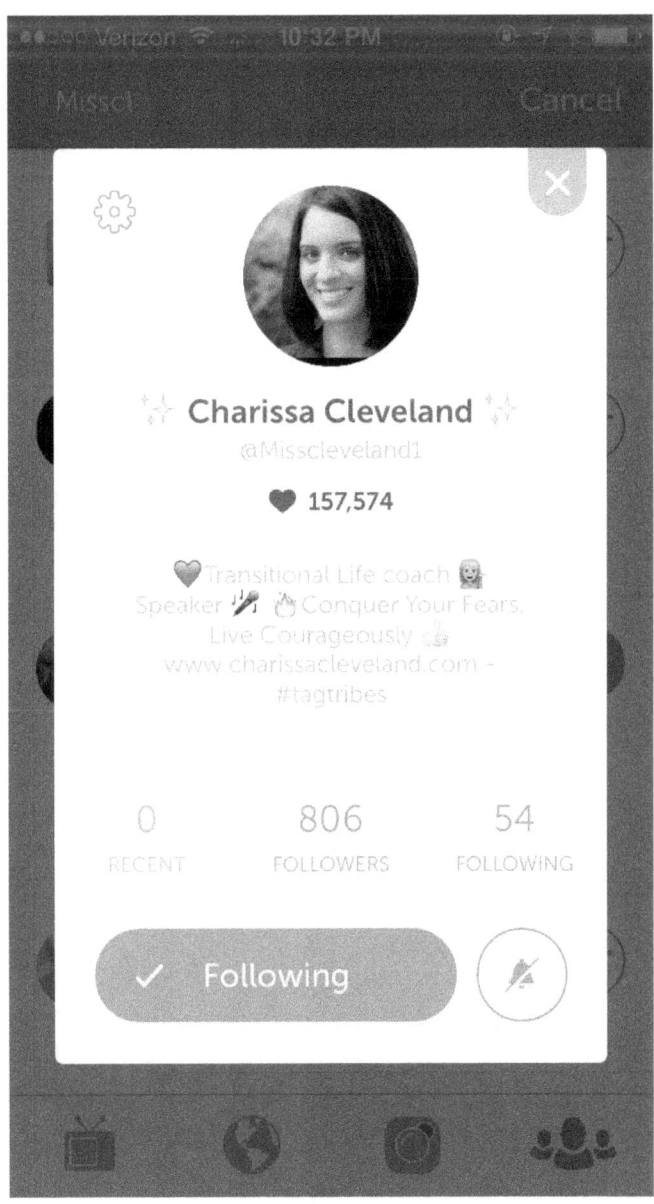

is a life coach based out of Sunny Phoenix, AZ who spends time in between motivating people to also share about what's going on in her life.

Section 6:
Periscope ads/Featured Broadcasts

Periscope ads is a mysterious new frontier for the platform.

Chapter 28 – Advertising

Post-Periscope Summit – after hearing from Alex Pettitt – I will go with his assumption –as he is privy to more inside information than 99.9% of Periscopers and agree with him when he says they have not yet introduced advertising to the platform (at least not officially) instead they "Featured" periscopers who the team at Periscope really likes and enjoys.

So [as of now] anyone can join the ranks of the awesome Featured periscopers – they just need to do something awesome. I actually clicked on one of these scopes for the first time to test Alex's theory and it seems to hold true. It was a minute long Periscope –the 'scoper was definitely not on the top of the Most loved list and he simply lined up three rubber chickens against the wall and after a few followers piled in – he pressed the rubber chickens and they made a funny sound. That was it. So yeah, do something goofy and awesome on Periscope and cross your fingers you may become an instant celebrity.

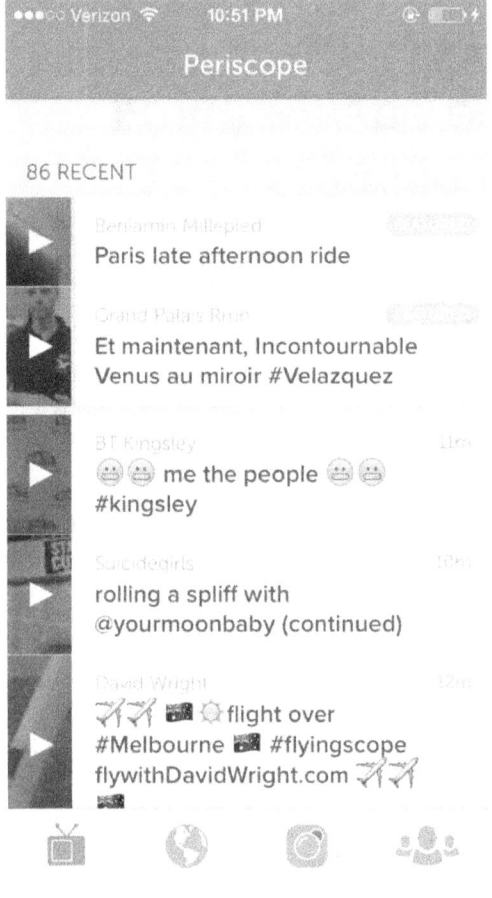

The ones that say "Featured" in Yellow are Periscope ads.

Section 7: Periscope Miscellanea

In this section we will discuss other things surrounding periscope but not necessarily related to how you would Periscope or watch a broadcast.

Chapter 29 –

Blocking fools & why it's important

For a while, a very short while, Periscope was an almost pristine online community where community members would watch others scopes on everything from their gym trip, to their dog's Halloween costume to their 3-year old's latest nasal cavity discovery.

However, this idyllic version of Periscope lasted only a matter of weeks before the online community of trolls arrived and began doing what it is trolls do – being annoying and ruining things.

Luckily for you and me it is fairly easy to block a troll on Periscope. All you really need to do is wait for the offending troll's offensive comment to pop-up. Click or tap on their name and then their profile should pull up.

When their profile pulls up – make sure to choose the "block" option and they will no longer enter your streams.

Chapter 30 - Online viewing sites

If you would like to view broadcasts online instead of on your IPhone or Android device you can do so by using one of these great websites:

1) Periscope Streams – www.onperiscope.com
   This site allows you to view a list of the different broadcasts that are showing on periscope at the current moment without logging into your periscope account through your phone.

   As expected though, since you are not logged into the Periscope app you cannot interact with the broadcaster or the other audience members.
2) Twitter – As of June 23rd 2015 - broadcasts now live on Twitter for replay as well as the actual broadcasts. One drawback is that you have to look at Twitter accounts individually to see what is going on with the broadcast.

   You also can't interact like you could if you were logged into your Periscope account.

3) Dextro Stream - http://stream.dextro.co/#/
   Dextro is a little bit different from onperiscope.com and Twitter itself in that it is so robust and quite possibly a marketers dream.

   Not only does the website allow you to view other streams but it also see what types of streams – i.e. "talking heads" or "People/Crowds" to see what has been the most broadcasted and also the most viewed in the past week and also on the current day.

Chapter 31 - Legal & Illegal Periscoping

Given that Periscope had thousands watching and likely hundreds broadcasting the now famous Mayweather – Pacquiao fight using the app – what's legal and illegal on periscope is up for debate.

According to the Periscope community guidelines as of this writing read:

"There are a few guidelines intended to keep Periscope open and safe:

- Do not post pornographic or overtly sexual content
- Do not publish explicitly graphic content or media that is intended to incite violent, illegal or dangerous activities
- Respect one another. Do not abuse, harass or post others' private, confidential information
- Do not impersonate to mislead or deceive
- Do not spam ."

So obviously this rules out porn site operators and rabble rousers looking to promote hate, violence or broadcast violence but a few other areas are still a murky area for the site. Two areas in particular are:

Sporting Events

This includes the big fight mentioned above. It also goes for any professional or amateur sporting events that may be broadcast using the app.

Check out this great article:

http://www.washingtonpost.com/business/economy/new-apps-threaten-tv-networks-golden-egg-live-sports/2015/05/05/b5d0b836-f347-11e4-84a6-6d7c67c50db0_story.html

Many sports organizations have condemned the app and made a policy of banning people using the app including the NHL and the PGA and currently the NFL. This is likely due to all of income these organizations make from their advertisers who see professional sports broadcast as a "captive audience".

However as people begin to learn more about the app and adopt it – it may become harder and harder to police someone holding their phone up at a game and determine the difference between someone using their phone to photograph the game and those using it to periscope.

Entertainment Events

Entertainers have been a little bit more relaxed on having their image taken at events as Katy Perry – one of the most followed Twitter users at this writing - was one of the first major musicians to periscope on the day it came out.

Personal Privacy

Finally personal privacy is a big concern these days and I for one want to share my two cents on this subject:

Privacy – as you knew it - is Dead.

I'll repeat – personal privacy is dead – it passed away the moment Meerkat and then Periscope arrived on the scene in a world that will likely have 2 billion smart phones not **cell phones** but *smart* **phones** by 2016. When a quarter (¼)of the world's population has the ability to both see what others are doing across the globe and broadcast what they are seeing privacy is dead.

That being said there are still developing countries like my wife's original home - Papua New Guinea – where smart phones are not widely used and few likely use the Periscope app (I've yet to see PNG show up on the Map function – this may change in coming months – especially if we go to visit)

An area that concerns me is the exposure or inadvertent overexposure of children – think soccer games, peewee football, your 4year old's birthday party where someone unskilled in the app is broadcasting to an estranged parent or worst a cyberstalker.

The negative aspects of the app can be explored extensively but in contrast so can the positive aspects. The app already allows others to experience what is happening across the globe the moment it happens and more people are becoming conscious of the fact that we are all just people.

I won't wax on much farther than to say wouldn't it be great to read someday "Persicope [or Meerkat] found to be driving factor in current state of world peace". That's a headline I will keep looking out for regardless.

Chapter 32 – Android vs IOS – Navigation

iOS – iOS was the first operating system for Periscope. For a long while (2 whole months) you could only use Periscope if you had an Apple IPhone or an IPad.

Then on May 26th – the Periscope Team released the Android version and millions signed up.

On both IOS and Android there are 4 main navigation icons. Those icons are the **TV**, the **Globe**, the **Monocle** and the **Three Amigos**.

1) **The TV** – this is where you can find replays and live broadcasts of those you subscribe to and also suggestions of those you follow.

2) **The Globe** – this is where you can find Periscope broadcasts that are active and live currently. You can do this one of two ways.

> a) You can use the Map function, on either device now, to see exactly where broadcasters (who have their location turned on) are broadcasting from.

> b) You can use the list function to see what the most popular Periscopes at this exact moment. The most viewed broadcast will be showing at the top of the list.

3) **The Monocle/Broadcast button** – this is button you press right before you're about to broadcast.

4) **The Three Amigos** – This is the Navigation feature that allows you to follow those you are following on Twitter, follow those who are leading in hearts aka the "Most loved" list it also is the gateway to looking at statistics in your own periscoping and how to adjust your settings.

iOS – On IOS all of the Navigation buttons are located on the bottom of the screen.

Android – On Android most of the Navigation buttons are located at the top of the screen. That includes The TV, The Globe and the Three Amigos.

The key difference is that on the bottom of the screen is where the **Monocle** or **Broadcast** button is. This button toggles back and forth between Broadcast and the magnifying glass/search function depending on which ICON you have selected at the top.

For example if the TV or Globe are selected the **monocle** is the default selection on the bottom. If the three amigos are selected at the top the Monocle transforms into the magnifying Glass/Search function.

Chapter 33

Android vs IOS – Which is Better?

SO a few months back when I began helping members of @sevennetworking—a locally headquartered networking group with chapters across the country. When Karen Joseph the founder of Seven (www.s-e-v-en.org) began periscoping about 2 months ago at this point—she was broadcasting from the most updated Samsung galaxy phone and she broadcasted her meetings to demonstrate the new app and it was uniformly agreed by the members that the quality was not as good as when I broadcasted from my IPhone. When she began broadcasting from a newly purchased IPad the quality dramatically improved. Another case study in this contrast is when I bought an android phone about 2.5 months ago so that I could train and accurately navigate the android platform. The moment I began broadcasting from the android phone my comments immediately began veering in the direction of "What's wrong with your phone" . When I asked what broadcast was better IPhone or Android—comments came back a unanimous "IPhone" for those who had seen my scopes before.

Here is what an android screen looks like:

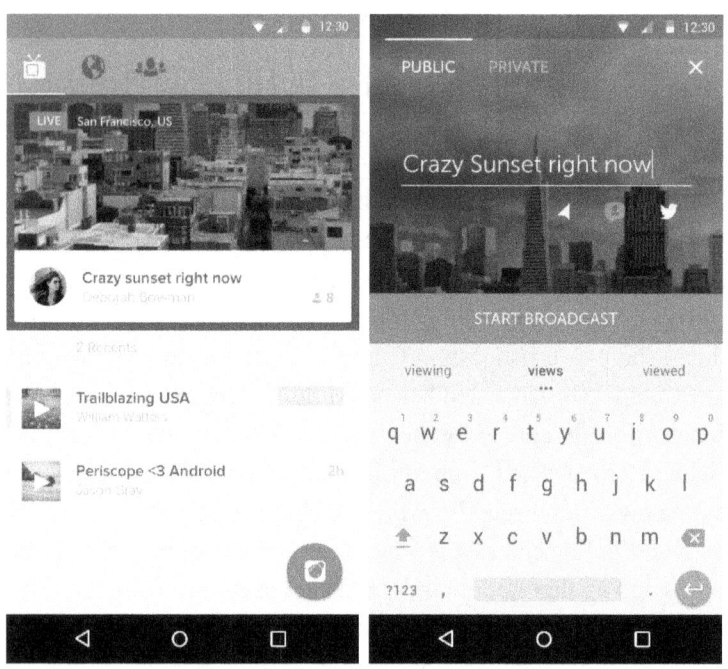

As you can see –they only have 3 icons at the top. The 4th is located at the bottom.

Chapter 34
Meerkat vs Periscope comparison

Real quick – I'll share my two cents on the Meerkat vs Periscope debate.

I've used both services and my experience on Meerkat is typically that I get on wait about 5 minutes for someone to view my broadcast and then as quickly as that one person enters my broadcast, they leave again.

My experience on Periscope is that 5 seconds after I begin broadcasting there is typically someone joining in and interacting with me in some way.

I do know that some people really enjoy Meerkat and others have even built up a substantial following on the platform so only time will tell which platform will do the best in the end.

Update: After speaking to a few Meerkasters face to face on the new platform blab.im – I've learned that there is definitely a different demographic on Meerkat that contrasts with those on Periscope. Meerkasters tend to watch longer and prefer longer form broadcasts.

So if you are broadcasting a very short minute long fireworks display you may want to choose periscope.

If you are broadcasting a filibuster on the congressional floor – you may want to use Meerkat.

Chapter 35 - Celebrities and Periscope

So one thing you'll notice after being on Periscope a while is that those with huge Twitter followings have a head start on those who have little to no Twitter followers.

About the only Celebrities I follow with any enthusiasm are business celebrities and the most active business celebrities on Periscope at this juncture are the members of Shark tank – especially Daymond John [@thesharkdaymond] and Kevin O'Leary [@kevinolearytv] who both got on the platform rather early.

One thing celebrities must be careful of is to never activate the location option (especially if they are in L.A.) because this will give people and stalkers an exact bead of what street corner they are nearest to.

Chapter 36 – What did I miss?

Landscape! SO the week of 9/7/15 Periscope released the long –awaited landscape version of periscope. It's great for Tourscopers and others as well. In order to broadcast via Landscape all one needs to do is simply tilt your phone horizontally as you broadcast.

Periscope sites: Now you can have your own periscope page online that shows your livestreams and broadcasts replays for up to 24 Hours.

Katch.me – Katch.me is an application you can register for that will allow you to save your streams using their service. This is a great way to keep your streams longer than 24 hours. This great service for Meerkat as well.

There is little doubt in my mind that this guide left out one or 100 great features or tidbits about the Periscope app or using the app for business that failed to wonder into my consciousness as I was writing this book.

So I can make this a complete guide I reserve this chapter for YOU. Tweet me a good point or update at @carteblancheme that I missed about Periscope and I will gladly mention you, your Twitter handle and website (or plug – within reason) along with your tip in a potential update to this edition.

Thank you for reading.

Bibliography – Great Articles on Periscope

Here's How Periscope Might Become a Real 'Thing' for Business
http://www.huffingtonpost.com/beverly-macy/heres-how-periscope-might_b_7532026.html
Meerkat VS Periscope – 7 Powerful Ways to Use Live-Streaming for Business
http://appdataroom.com/meerkat-vs-periscope-7-powerful-ways-to-use-live-streaming-for-business/
Six Business Uses for Periscope
http://todmaffin.com/periscope-for-business
How to Use Periscope for Business
http://www.deepspacemarketing.com/periscope-for-business/
As Business Tools, Meerkat and Periscope Fall Way Short Of Google Hangouts On Air
(for the record I disagree with this article)
http://www.forbes.com/sites/quickerbettertech/2015/03/30/how-twitter-helps-madonna-sell-songs-while-google-helps-davita-save-kidneys/
How To Use Periscope To Grow Your Ecommerce Business
http://www.shopify.com/blog/33559876-how-to-use-periscope-to-grow-your-ecommerce-business
How to Use Meerkat and Periscope for Business
http://www.digitalbusinessacademyuk.com/how-use-meerkat-and-periscope-business
5 Ways Brands Can Use Periscope and Meerkat
http://www.entrepreneur.com/article/247005
Why live video streaming is the next big thing
http://www.citigatedewerogerson.com/cdr-blog/live-video-streaming-next-big-thing/#more-850
How to Use Periscope for Your Business
http://strategicrevolution.com/how-to-use-periscope-for-your-business
6 Ways to Use Live Streaming Video for Business
http://www.socialmediaexaminer.com/live-streaming-video-for-business/
How You Can Use Hot New Apps Meerkat and Periscope - For Business
https://www.linkedin.com/pulse/how-you-can-use-hot-new-apps-

meerkat-periscope-business-ryan-holmes

5 Quick Tips for Using Periscope, Twitter's New Live Video Streaming App

http://blog.hubspot.com/marketing/periscope-app-live-broadcasting-tips

http://www.brw.com.au/p/marketing/live_streaming_apps_periscope_and_KQgDzNAUU3K9ed4mRyTsHJ

Here's how Periscope, Twitter's live streaming app, could transform your business

https://www.visioncritical.com/periscope/

How to use Periscope on Android, and why you'd want to. What is Periscope - Periscope FAQ - live-streaming app

http://www.pcadvisor.co.uk/how-to/google-android/how-use-periscope-on-android-3613985/

Periscope arrives on Android with a few features that you can't get on the iPhone

http://www.businessinsider.com/periscope-now-on-android-2015-5

Periscope Terms of Service:

https://www.periscope.tv/tos

Mayweather – P fight:

http://www.theverge.com/2015/5/3/8539483/periscope-made-it-easy-to-watch-the-mayweather-pacquiao-fight-for-free

Washington POST – live sports + Periscope article:

http://www.washingtonpost.com/business/economy/new-apps-threaten-tv-networks-golden-egg-live-sports/2015/05/05/b5d0b836-f347-11e4-84a6-6d7c67c50db0_story.html

2 billion smart phones

http://www.emarketer.com/Article/2-Billion-Consumers-Worldwide-Smartphones-by-2016/1011694

Periscope Now Has 10 Million users Who Watch 21 Million Minutes a Day

http://www.adweek.com/news/technology/periscope-now-has-10-million-users-who-watch-21-million-minutes-day-166361